D1093937

The Heritage Book 1989

Edna McCann

Collier Macmillan Canada, Inc.

Collier Macmillan Canada, Inc.
1200 Eglinton Ave. East, Suite 200
Don Mills, Ontario   M3C 3N1

ISBN 02.953526.3

Printed and bound in Canada

Thirteenth Edition

PICTURE CREDITS

INTRODUCTION

This is the thirteenth year that I have composed this little book. Many people consider the number thirteen to be unlucky, but this year I feel rather fortunate indeed. For once again I have the opportunity to share my experiences and my books with you. I am always delighted to learn of people who were cheered by a humorous anecdote or inspired by the beauty of a poet's vision.

There is nothing so gratifying as the bridges we build to our fellow human beings. In this last year of the decade, and as the new century approaches, many of us are becoming more aware of how hard life in the world is for many people. I have also found that more and more people are giving of themselves to help others in need, whether they be next door or in another country.

With all the rapid changes in the world, how comforting it is to rely on the warmth of family bonds and the strength of God's love. And how wonderful it is to laugh with friends in happy times!

In the spirit of togetherness I offer you *The Heritage Book 1989* with the hope that every day will bring you joy.

Edna McCann

January

A Prayer for the New Year

L ORD God of Eternity, we give Thee thanks
for the gift of this new year. Give us grace
to use it day by day in loving concern for all
that thou hast created, through Jesus Christ,
Our Lord. Amen.

A new year is a gracious gift. It is a time to
look back and honestly appraise our use of the
year just ended. It is a time to dream dreams
that will express our most precious hopes for
others. It is a time to make new resolutions and
to start day by day to make them real in our
own lives and through us, real in the lives of
others. Let us make this a truly happy new
year.

Monday — January 2

IF we can say with Seneca "This life is only a prelude to eternity" then we need not worry so much over the fittings and furnishings of this ante room; and more than that, it will give dignity and purpose to the fleeting days to know they are linked with the eternal things as prelude and preparation.

— *Savage*

Tuesday — January 3

JAMIE and Marshall's wedding, Christmas, the holiday week, and New Year's were all such emotional and happy times that I am feeling somewhat drained. I need some time to "charge my battery" as it were.

Isn't it strange that times of great joy can be as physically and mentally tiring as times of trouble or sadness?

I have found that a few days of quiet reading, pleasant music, and good cups of tea will refresh and revitalize me.

THE HERITAGE BOOK

THE snow and winds of the past few days have left many giant drifts around the house. Marg and I enjoy our evening walks but I think we will have to forego our trek. Grace Noll Crowell wrote this lovely poem, "A Wintry Mile" and this evening I will imagine my walk.

Walk a mile in the winter twilight,
Mark its whiteness and breathe its cold,
Reach your hand to the sunset embers,
Warm them there, and when you are old
There will be times when you recall it:
A beautiful, perfect, shining while,
That will glow in your heart like a
    splendid diamond —
You will remember that winter mile.
You will recall the clean cold stinging
Of winter wind on your throat and lips,
The lift of your heart in its youthful gladness,
The tingle of blood to your fingertips;
You will have drawn to your heart forever
This hour, the snow, the light in the west —
Walk awhile in the winter twilight,
Store its treasures within your breast.

THURSDAY — JANUARY 5

TRUE friendship is of royal lineage. It is of the same kith and breeding as loyalty and self-forgetting devotion and proceeds upon a higher principle even than they. For loyalty may be blind, and friendship must not be; devotion may sacrifice principles of right choice which friendship must guard with an excellent and watchful care — The object of love is to serve, not to win.

— *Woodrow Wilson*

FRIDAY — JANUARY 6

ONE of the loveliest stories associated with the birth of Jesus Christ is the adoration of the Wise Men. Here were the first gentiles to acknowledge the uniqueness of this child. In many church traditions this day is commemorated by acknowledging that Christ is the Messiah (the sent one) for people of all races, cultures, and nationalities.

In Christ's presence all people are of equal worth. In His worship all are bound in common love and loyalty.

THE HERITAGE BOOK

MARSHALL and his new bride Jamie returned from their honeymoon last evening. Marg, my son-in-law Bruce, and I were delighted to see them today and to hear about their wonderful holiday.

The young couple had spent many hours before their marriage deciding how they wished to spend their honeymoon. Finally, since both are avid skiers, they chose to visit one of Canada's finest ski areas — Whistler, British Columbia.

After a pleasant flight from Toronto to Vancouver they rented a car to drive north to Whistler Mountain. The small village was built right at the foot of the mountain and the hotels and inns all have glorious views of the snow-capped peaks.

The ski runs are serviced by chair lifts and gondolas, and the runs are suited to all skiing types, from novices to experts.

It was a wonderful holiday and certainly a honeymoon to remember.

THE HERITAGE BOOK

IT happened at this time that Jesus came from Nazareth to Galilee and was baptized in the Jordan by John. At the moment when he came up out of the water, he saw the heavens torn open and the spirit, like a dove, descending upon him. And a voice spoke from heaven "Thou art my Son, my Beloved, on whom my favour rests."

— Mark 1: 9–11

MY good friend Jake Frampton stopped by for dinner last evening. He brought his V.C.R. (a Christmas present given to him by his young nephews) and several tapes that he thought we might enjoy together.

The first was a travelogue from Venice, Italy, a very interesting film. The second was a Sunday night concert from Symphony Hall in Boston, Massachusetts.

It was truly magnificent to see Mr. Davis, the conductor, and his musicians perform without the usual commercial interruptions. Modern technology never ceases to amaze me.

TUESDAY — JANUARY 10

MANY years ago my husband George and I spent one winter in Montreal. What I remember most from that time are the sleighs. No other city in Canada had such a rich variety of commercial sleighs — the coal man's, the "Frites" or chips sleigh, the fruit and vegetable peddler's sleigh, the ragpicker's, and many more.

Most Montrealers with cars usually put them up on blocks because it was much too difficult to run them on the snow-covered streets. The old horse-drawn sleighs had the run of the streets!

The fruit and vegetable peddler's sleigh was quite unique. It was heated by a Quebec coal-burning heater and had a tiny chimney on the roof.

Another of my favourites was the "Frites" wagon. Their French-fried potatoes, served in paper cones, were the best ever!

THE most valuable of all talents is that of never using two words when one will do.

— *Thomas Jefferson*

ELEANOR Roosevelt always carried this prayer with her.

"Our Father, who has set a restlessness in our hearts and made us all seekers after that which we can never fully find, keep us at tasks too hard for us, that we may be driven to Thee for strength."

DO you feel a little edgy today? If you are nervous because it is a Friday and the date is the thirteenth you may be suffering from "triskaidekaphobia." Experts offer the opinion that this fear stems from the fact that there were thirteen people at the Last Supper, and that Christ's crucifixion occurred on a Friday.

I have no such fear so I guess I will spend today teasing my friends who do.

THE HERITAGE BOOK

SATURDAY — JANUARY 14

IT is easy to be pleasant
When life flows by like a song
But the man worth while is one who will smile,
When everything goes dead wrong.
For the test of the heart is trouble,
And it always comes with the years
And the smile that is worth the praises of earth
Is the smile that shines thru the tears.

SUNDAY — JANUARY 15

THE word of God became flesh and dwelt among us. To all who received Him gave He the power to become the Children of God.
— *John 1*

MONDAY — JANUARY 16

YESTERDAY was the birthdate of Martin Luther King Jr., the late inspirational leader of black Americans.

"When you are right you cannot be too radical; when you are wrong, you cannot be too conservative."

THE HERITAGE BOOK

I have always enjoyed reading mystery novels and one of my favourite authors is John D. MacDonald. His sense of character and his skilful descriptions of every sort of person, setting, and event give credibility to all his novels and short stories.

Mr. MacDonald was born in Sharon, Pennsylvania in 1916. After graduation from university he married Dorothy Prentiss. It was she who typed his first short story and submitted it to *Story Magazine*. It appeared in the July-August 1946 issue.

In the next four years he wrote hundreds of magazine stories and in 1950 he had his first novel published. He wrote sixty-six novels in all, including twenty-one about his favourite character, Travis McGee.

MacDonald and his wife lived in Sarasota, Florida until his death in 1986. I'm sure his stories will endure for many generations of readers.

THE HERITAGE BOOK

A lot of people are like wheelbarrows — no good unless pushed. Some are like trailers — they have to be pulled. Some are like kites — if you don't keep a string on them, they will fly away. Some are like balloons — full of wind and ready to blow up. Some are like footballs — you can't tell which way they will bounce. And then, some are like a good watch — open-faced, pure gold, quietly busy, and full of good works.

SOMETIMES tests don't always show a child's intelligence.

To prove that point a grade one student was shown two pictures — one of a man chopping wood, the other of a man reading a book. The child was told to circle the drawing that showed "a man at work." The child circled the man reading the book and it was marked incorrect.

The tester had no way of knowing that the child's father was a teacher, who read books at work and chopped wood for relaxation.

Friday — January 20

COURAGE is resistance to fear, mastery of fear — not absence of fear.

— *Mark Twain*

Saturday — January 21

THE weather this winter has been particularly severe and I have been concerned about my feathered friends.

Today, Marg, my granddaughter Phyllis, and I made suet balls to hang on the tree branches, hoping in this small way to help the birds "weather the weather."

Suet is not very easy to come by these days. In my youth every wife and mother used suet when cooking a roast of beef, and the butcher always added extra chunks that we used to hang out for the birds.

Luckily Marg has an old friend whose neighbourhood butcher was able to give us some good, large pieces to use. We rolled the suet balls in wild bird seed and then tied the balls securely with string.

I felt much better as I snuggled in my bed to think that some birds will be warmer tonight because of our efforts.

Sunday — January 22

JESUS went round the whole of Galilee teaching in the synagogues, preaching the gospel of the kingdom and curing whatever illness or infirmity there was among the people. His fame reached the whole of Syria; and sufferers from every kind of illness, racked with pain, possessed by devils, epileptic or paralysed were all brought to Him and He cured them.

— Matthew 4: 23–24

Monday — January 23

MY son-in-law Bruce is a member of our local Rotary Club. The first Rotary Club in Canada was formed in Winnipeg in 1910. Today there are clubs in every province and territory with a membership of over thirty thousand.

The motto of the club is "Service Above Self." Worldwide, Rotarians contribute more than 350 million dollars annually to service many philanthropic projects.

Bruce is justifiably proud to be a member of this wonderful organization.

TUESDAY — JANUARY 24

IF you are planning for a year, sow rice.
If you are planning for a decade, plant trees.
If you are planning for a lifetime, educate a
person.

— Chinese Proverb

WEDNESDAY — JANUARY 25

TODAY is the birthdate of Robbie Burns, the
Scottish poet. My mother was very proud
of her Scottish ancestry and she instilled in us
this same pride.

Life is but a day at most,
Sprung from night, — in darkness lost:
Hope not sunshine ev'ry hour,
Fear not clouds will always lour.

THURSDAY — JANUARY 26

WHEN my husband George was at one of his first parishes he needed a new secretary. One of the ladies he interviewed was considerably older than he was.

"I see that your birthday is October ninth. What year?" asked George.

The lady looked at George sternly and answered with a sniff, "Every year, young man!"

She got the job.

FRIDAY — JANUARY 27

MY great-grandson Justin is becoming quite a handful for Bill and Phyllis. Today, Phyllis heard loud noises in the laundry room and when she rushed in Justin was calmly standing in front of a thumping dryer. Phyllis opened the door and out jumped Sandy, the family dog.

"Good heavens! What were you thinking of, Justin?"

His answer was typically Justin. "Well, I gave him a bath, he was cold and wet so I wanted to dry him fast and have him smell good."

SATURDAY — JANUARY 28

SOME good friends of Marshall and Jamie are looking at homes with the hope of buying something nice but within a reasonable price range. This is not an easy thing to do these days.

"Realestatese" is a new language that makes the description of the house bear as little resemblance as possible to its real appearance.

Here are a few examples.

Newly decorated: The owner has repainted the front door.

Needs finishing touches: No paint or paper or baseboards are anywhere to be seen.

Handyman's special: A handyman and $100,000 would make it habitable.

A charming smaller home: A single-car garage is larger.

SUNDAY — JANUARY 29

JESUS said "How blest you are when you suffer insults and persecution for my sake. Accept it with gladness and exaltation, for you have your reward in heaven."

— Matthew 5: 11–12

THE HERITAGE BOOK

I am fortunate, at my age, to still have my own teeth. I had my check-up today with Dr. Misener and he assured me that my teeth would "hang on for some time to come, Edna."

This pleased me immensely as I have always had a terrible fear of the dentist and of dental extractions in particular.

In early times, the most common treatment of diseased teeth was extraction. This procedure was done by one of three horrific methods. One was to loosen the tooth by applying caustics. Another was to insert a dry peppercorn into the cavity. The peppercorn would soon swell so large that it would break the tooth into pieces. Most commonly, the patient lay with his head between the doctor's knees while dental tongs rocked the tooth until it came out.

Thank goodness for modern dentistry.

TUESDAY — JANUARY 31

You cannot help men permanently by doing for them what they could and should do for themselves.

February

What matter if the chill winds bite and blow,
If things which once were fair are bleak and dead
If all of spring's sweet harbingers are fled,
If roses lie asleep 'neath piles of snow,
And streamlets, dark and cold, have ceased to flow?
I do not feel the blasts about my head;
I've known a breeze that kissed my cheek and said:
"Spring's come": I've heard the lark's song and I know
The quiet beauties of the dusk in May,
When daylight steals to keep its tryst with night.
I've waked at dawn at the sound of a bird's lay;
I've watched the silvery moon fade out of sight.
Remembering this, can I dread winter? Nay,
Spring's in my heart—when all the world is white.

— *Dorothy Van Dermeulen*

THE HERITAGE BOOK

<u>THURSDAY — FEBRUARY 2</u>

"WIARTON Willie" the groundhog saw his shadow today and if superstition is to be believed we are in for six more weeks of winter.

This has been a particularly harsh winter in our area, and so the radio forecast seemed especially discouraging today.

My grandson's wife June also heard the forecast and decided to do something to cheer up Marg and me. This afternoon she delivered two enormous bouquets of spring flowers. There were daffodils, tulips, and a variety of other bright cheerful flowers. Goodness knows where or at what dreadful expense she was able to find these bouquets but we deeply appreciated her thoughtfulness.

<u>FRIDAY — FEBRUARY 3</u>

THE light of friendship is like the light of phosphorous, seen plainest when all around it is dark.

— *Grace Noll Crowell*

SATURDAY — FEBRUARY 4

M^Y friend Mavis Tewbury is a truly amazing lady. Several years ago her grandchildren gave her a complete cross-country ski outfit. She was not a young woman but she decided to give the sport a try. At first she was quite nervous — it's not easy to fall when one is older — but as her skill increased she became more and more confident.

This year Mavis signed up for a cross-country ski trip to Vermont. She and another older friend have just returned home from a two-week vacation in that beautiful American state.

In her letter she wrote, "You know Edna, it was wonderful. We would get up in the morning, eat a hearty breakfast and then put on our skis for the day's trip. We would ski many miles along beautiful wooded trails. After lunch we skied on to the next inn on our tour. Then we would sightsee before a leisurely dinner. I have never enjoyed a holiday more!"

THE HERITAGE BOOK

JESUS said "I am the light of the world. No follower of mine shall wander in the darkness. He shall have the light of life."

— John 8: 12

I greatly admired the female aviator Amelia Earhart, and so I was delighted when I heard this story about her early years as a flyer.

In 1922 Miss Earhart had managed to save the princely sum of twenty dollars. With this money she bought an elegant leather jacket. She loved the jacket but decided that it looked too new. How were people to know she was a seasoned flyer when she was wearing a brand new aviator's jacket? She decided that what her jacket really needed was wrinkles.

Her solution? She slept in her new jacket for the next three nights.

"I must do something" will always solve more problems than "Something must be done."

THE HERITAGE BOOK

As we begin this lenten season I like to remember my husband George's favourite ideas for lent. George used one verse from Paul's letter to the Philippians that contains six positive thoughts.

"And now my friends, all that is true, all that is noble, all that is just and pure, all that is lovable and gracious, whatever is excellent and admirable—fill all your thoughts with these things." (*Phil. 4: 8*)

George suggested using one of these thoughts for each week of lent. It makes lent a very positive season.

Today's weather announcers give areas of low pressure and chances of snow or sun in percentages that often make it seem as if they are running a lottery.

At the end of these reports I am often left confused. So I was very happy to hear our local young forecaster announce this morning, "Snow today. Can't tell how much. It hasn't stopped yet."

THE HERITAGE BOOK

As I sat looking through an old picture album today I came, with delight, upon an old photo of our family about to climb aboard a train. What wonderful memories that faded picture evoked.

It was my first train ride. Sarah, Ben, and I were travelling with our parents all the way to Montreal to visit my Aunt Ethel, father's sister.

I remember how anxiously we had stood on the platform watching for the telltale smoke of our train.

Finally we were boarding. The conductor helped us up the steps and we headed into the train's interior. Father had reserved a dining table for us and oh, the luxury of it — white table cloths, silverware, good china, and a tall elegant waiter. I was almost too excited to eat.

Later, hidden behind the green velvet draw drapes of our berths, we snuggled into our pyjamas. Soon the rhythmic clickety-clack of the wheels and the swaying of the car put me into one of the deepest sleeps of my young life.

THE HERITAGE BOOK

SATURDAY — FEBRUARY 11

SOME men have their first dollar. The man who is really rich is the man who still has his first friend.

SUNDAY — FEBRUARY 12

OUT of the depths have I called you, O Lord.

Lord, hear my voice; Let your ears consider well the voice of my supplication.

I wait for the Lord, my soul waits for him, in his word is my hope.

O Israel wait for the Lord for with the Lord there is mercy.

— Psalm 130: 1-6

MONDAY — FEBRUARY 13

I enjoyed James Russell Lowell's views on country living.

"No man, I suspect, ever lived long in the country without being bitten by these meteorological ambitions. He likes to be hotter and colder, to have been more deeply snowed up to, to have more trees and larger blown down than his neighbours."

THE HERITAGE BOOK

MAY the skies above be cloudless
On this February day,
May the sun beam warm and golden
As it shines along your way.

May your problems find solution,
May vexations not arise,
And may all the joy of living
Be reflected in your eyes.

May the dreams and hopes you've cherished
Find fulfillment very soon,
And may all your world be happy
As birds sing a joyous tune.

May God's blessings rest upon you,
And may everything you see
Make you know how much I love you,
And how much you mean to me.

This lovely poem "Valentine Wishes"
was written by Alice Kennelly Roberts.

On this Valentine's Day I hope that each of
you may have "the joy of living reflected in
your eyes."

THE HERITAGE BOOK

MY friend Jake Frampton is the owner of a lovely little book store and as such his interest in books and authors is very keen.

Jake told me a most interesting anecdote about *Paradise Lost*, John Milton's famous work.

It took Milton more than seven years from 1658 to 1665 to compose his poem. He sold the manuscript for the immediate payment of five pounds or roughly twenty-five dollars. Two years passed before the sale of the first edition, when Milton received a total of nearly fifty dollars for his masterpiece.

In the year 1681 Milton's widow sold all the rights to the book for eight pounds or forty dollars.

All things considered, I guess you could say that Milton was in the ranks of underpaid authors.

PEACE is not the absence of conflict but the ability to cope with it.

FRIDAY — FEBRUARY 17

TIME heals griefs and quarrels for we change and are no longer the same persons. Neither the offender nor the offended are any more themselves. It is like a nation which we have provoked, but meet again after two generations. They are still Frenchmen but not the same.

— *Blaise Pascal*

SATURDAY — FEBRUARY 18

I dwell in Possibility —
A fairer house than Prose —
More numerous of Windows —
Superior — for Doors.

— *Emily Dickinson*

SUNDAY — FEBRUARY 19

OUR souls await the Lord. He is our help and our shield.
Indeed our heart rejoices in him for in his holy name we put our trust.
Let your loving kindness, O Lord, be upon us as we put our trust in thee.

— *Psalm 33: 20–22*

THE HERITAGE BOOK

MY dear friend Emily winters in Florida. She has a lovely condominium in the St. Petersburg area and receives many guests. In her latest letter she writes, "Having as much company as I do Edna, I have come up with thoughts on how to be the perfect guest.

"The perfect guest treats my home as their own during their stay. They look for things to do to be helpful and they do them.

"The perfect guest is an interesting conversationalist. They show an interest in my friends and neighbours here and don't always talk about people that only we know to the exclusion of others in our company.

"The perfect guest helps out with the expense of groceries and on occasion says 'I'll do dinner tonight'.

"But the really perfect guest knows when to say good-bye."

Tuesday — February 21

SOME critics are like chimney sweepers: they put out the fire below, or frighten the swallows from their nests above; they scrape a long time in the chimney, cover themselves with soot, and bring nothing away but a bag of cinders, and then sing from the top of the house as if they had built it.

— Henry Wadsworth Longfellow

Wednesday — February 22

IT isn't the money you are making,
It isn't the clothes you wear;
It isn't the skill of your good right hand
That makes folks really care.
But it's the smile on your face
And the burdens that you bear;
It's how do you live, and neighbour,
It's how do you work and play,
And it's how do you say "Good Morning"
To the people along the way;
And it's how do you face your troubles
Whenever the skies are gray.

— Byrne

THE HERITAGE BOOK

M Y daughter Mary and her husband John came for dinner this evening. John is a minister so free evenings are rare indeed.

John was telling me, over our supper, how a computer has changed his life. He has spent many hours transferring biblical text references and other biblical information onto a computer. As well, he has added many of my late husband George's sermons and reference material.

The computer files now enable him to locate biblical references that can be used for specific events or special days in the church without the hours of manual research.

John even writes his sermons on a word processor. With this amazing machine he can add or delete material, rearrange paragraphs and, in the end, have a good, clear sermon that is easy to deliver.

"You know, Mother, I am really enjoying my life as a pastor so much more. I have greater confidence in my sermons and my ability to deliver them. Maybe this use is what the good Lord had in mind when he gave us computers."

THE HERITAGE BOOK

MISFORTUNES one can endure — they come from outside; they are accidents. But to suffer for one's own faults — ah, there is the sting of life.

— *Oscar Wilde*

THE first man who, having fenced in a piece of land, said, "This is mine," and found people naive enough to believe him, that man was the true founder of civil society.

— *Jean Jacques Rousseau*

COME let us sing to the Lord, let us shout for joy to the rock of our salvation.

Let us come before his presence with thanks-giving and raise a loud shout to him with psalms.

For the Lord is a great God and a great king above all gods.

— *Psalm 95: 1–3*

Monday — February 27

M Y young neighbour David stopped by last evening for a visit. Just over a year ago David was diagnosed as having cancer. Since then he has undergone a series of chemo-therapy treatments, enduring the loss of his hair and other serious side effects. But last night he was in great humour.

He had returned Saturday from his latest check-up and the doctors were thrilled. It appears that young David's cancer has been cured. Although no cancer patient is considered "cured" until five years have passed cancer-free there is no further sign of the life-threatening disease.

Tonight as I went to bed I said a special thank you to God for this young boy's life.

Tuesday — February 28

O NE of the hardest things to teach children about money matters is that it does.

March

WEDNESDAY — MARCH 1

THESE are the things I prize
  And hold of dearest worth:
Light of the sapphire skies,
Peace of the silent hills,
Shelter of the forests, comfort of the grass,
Music of the birds, murmur of little rills,
Shadow of clouds that swiftly pass,
And, after showers,
The smell of flowers
And of the good brown earth —
And best of all, along the way,
Friendship and mirth.

THURSDAY — MARCH 2

SOME years ago a man complained to his pastor that the church was constantly asking for money.

"It seems to be always give, give, give," he said. The minister smiled and replied "You know, that is one of the best definitions of Christianity that I have ever heard."

THE HERITAGE BOOK

I am so pleased that March has finally arrived. It is good to be in a month that has spring in it. With all the snow this winter I have found it difficult to get about. I still enjoy a winter's walk but even the sidewalks have been treacherous and at my age I don't like to risk a bad spill.

My good friends Will and Muriel stopped by today with an amusing tale about winter's slippery footing.

They had been walking across an extremely icy parking lot when an elderly lady slipped and fell, scattering her small bag of groceries. Will hurried over to help her up while Muriel picked up her packages. Just as she got to her feet the lady slipped again, knocking Will's feet out from under him. Will in turn knocked Muriel down and the three of them wound up sitting in the lot with parcels scattered everywhere. Another gentleman called over, "Shall I come and help or shall I just call a tow truck?"

Eventually they all managed to get up and fortunately no one was injured.

Ah, the perils of winter.

SATURDAY — MARCH 4

IF I can put one touch of a rosy sunset into the life of any man or woman, I shall feel that I have worked with God.

— Henry David Thoreau

SUNDAY — MARCH 5

"AND now my friends think on all that is lovable, amicable and deserving love; think on the beauty of the earth for it was created for love and by love, behold the beauty of the soul, the fullest expression of God's love.

God loved the world so much that He gave his only son that everyone who has faith in Him may not die but have eternal life."

MONDAY — MARCH 6

IN a time when most people buy things on the installment plan it was refreshing to see this sign in a furniture store window.

"Try our easy payment plan. 100% down. No future worries about payments."

THE HERITAGE BOOK

TODAY I visited my good friend Lila McGuiness who is in hospital recovering from minor surgery. During my visit one of the hospital volunteers told us that visiting hours would soon be over, but because Mrs. McGuiness had no relatives in the area and had few visitors she would just quietly shut our door and leave us to chat.

I couldn't help but compare this volunteer with another that I met at a hospital in Buffalo, New York, where I had gone to visit a dear friend who was dying.

This volunteer was giving out the passes required to visit in the intensive care unit. When we asked for a pass she replied, "I'm doing some paper work—come back later." Startled, we complied. Shortly we asked again and she snapped, "I'm sure it's not visiting hours yet, stop bothering me."

Thankfully such volunteers are *not* the norm.

THE HERITAGE BOOK

TODAY is my son-in-law's birthday. Marg baked his favourite cake — chocolate with chocolate icing. After a festive birthday dinner Marg brought in the cake ablaze with candles for Bruce to blow out.

As we ate our cake and sipped our tea Bruce explained that the custom of celebrating a birthday by blowing out candles originated in ancient Greece. Worshippers of the moon goddess Artemis celebrated her birthday by placing honey cakes with lighted candles on their altars.

Eventually the ancient Greeks began placing lighted candles on cakes to celebrate children's birthdays too — and added the practice of blowing out the candles. They believed burning candles had mystical powers, and that if a child made a wish and blew out all the candles with one puff his or her wish would be granted.

FROM the days of the first grandfather, everybody has remembered a golden age behind him.

THE HERITAGE BOOK

IDEALS are like stars; you will not succeed in touching them with your hands. But like the seafaring man on the desert of waters, you choose them as your guides, and following them you will reach your destiny.

— *Carl Shurz*

MY great-grandson Mickey is an "everything" collector. He keeps his collections in old shoe boxes. It is driving his mother June to distraction.

On our last visit to their country home I was discussing Mickey's collections with him. I discovered that one of his shoe boxes was full of used bubblegum, old pieces that had all the flavour chewed out of them.

"Mickey, I'm wondering why you would want to save old bubble gum."

"I'm not sure yet either, Gran," was his reply, "but I'll be happy to tell you the minute I know."

Sunday — March 12

Yea, though I walk through the valley of the shadow of death, I will fear no evil, for thou art with me, thy rod and thy staff they comfort me.

— Psalm 23: 4

Monday — March 13

I have always loved cheese. As a child it was a budget stretcher for our family. Mother always had a large block of cheddar on hand for cheese omelettes, grilled cheese sandwiches, egg and cheese pie (now more elegantly known as quiche) and father's favourite, fried cheese.

Cheese has been made in different forms for hundreds of years. Legend has it that some four thousand years ago an Arabian merchant put his milk supply in a pouch before he set off across the desert. At nightfall, after hours in the blazing sun, he found that the milk in the pouch had separated into curds and whey. The whey satisfied his thirst and the curds, his hunger.

One of my favourite cheeses is goat's milk cheese. Whatever your favourite, cheese is not only delicious but healthful as well.

THE HERITAGE BOOK

I have never had the pleasure of visiting the Orient but I enjoyed it vicariously as my daughter Julia showed us slides of her recent trip.

She had to travel to Thailand on a business trip so she took an extra two weeks of holiday time and toured Singapore, Malacca, Kuala Lumpur, Penang, and the countryside in all these areas. She found it to be a fascinating experience.

Julia and her travelling companion felt it prudent to hire a guide, and this proved to be the wisest of ideas. With the guide they visited temples and native homes, and were able to learn about the people and their customs by being with them.

The local people in their turn were fascinated by Julia and her friend. Were they (females) really permitted to travel alone? Was it possible that they were company executives?

It was a learning experience for all of them and a trip that Julia will not soon forget.

WEDNESDAY — MARCH 15

Bring unto the sorrowing,
All release from pain;
Let the lips of Laughter
Overflow again.
And with all the needy,
O divide, I pray,
This vast treasure of content
That is mine today!
— *James Whitcomb Riley*

THURSDAY — MARCH 16

THE wise man looks inside his heart and finds eternal peace.
— *Hindu Proverb*

FRIDAY — MARCH 17

TODAY is St. Patrick's day — the day for the "wearin' o' the green."

My father was of Irish background and he revelled in the celebration of this day. His favourite proverb was "May you be in Heaven an hour before the Devil knows you're gone."

THE HERITAGE BOOK

THREE-year-old Louis loved to play in his father's saddle-making shop in the French village of Coupvray.

One day Louis quietly picked up two of his father's sharp awls and left the shop. Hurrying along he fell and was struck in the eyes by the awls. At that moment Louis Braille became totally blind.

When he was ten his parents sent him to the school for the blind in Paris. The founder, Valentin Huay, had invented a system to enable blind people to "read" with their fingers by using cut-out letters of cloth pasted on pages. However, each letter was enormous and this method was impractical.

In 1836, when Louis was twenty-seven, he had perfected his own system of raised dots and dashes that were written with an awl.

Isn't it strange that the instrument that caused Louis Braille's blindness was the same instrument that allowed him to give reading and writing to blind people around the world.

THE HERITAGE BOOK

Palm Sunday

THE glory of our King was seen
  when he came riding by
And all the children waved and sang
  Hosanna, King most high,
The glory of our King was seen when
  with his arms stretched wide
To show his love to everyone, Jesus
  was crucified.
The glory of our King was seen on the
  first Easter day
When Christ rose up, set free from
  death, to love, to guide, to stay.
                    — *Margaret B. Cropper*

How beautiful it is to do nothing,
and then to rest afterward.
                    — *Spanish Proverb*

You can't get anywhere today if you are still
mired down in yesterday.

WEDNESDAY — MARCH 22

Spring! Spring, spring, spring! My heart has been singing that word all day today. I know that there is very little in the weather to indicate that this glorious season is upon us but at least I can look at the calendar and feel great joy!

John Greenleaf Whittier's poem speaks beautifully of spring.

Close to my heart I fold each lovely thing
The sweet day yields; and not disconsolate,
With the calm patience of the woods I wait
For leaf and blossom when God gives us
    Spring!

THURSDAY — MARCH 23

There are one-story intellects, two-story intellects and three-story intellects with skylights. All fact collectors, who have no aim beyond their facts, are one-story men. Two-story men compare reason, generalize, using the labours of the fact collectors as well as their own. Three-story men idealize, imagine, predict; their best illumination comes from above, through the skylight.

— *Oliver Wendell Holmes*

Friday — March 24

Good Friday

GOOD Friday always had special meaning for George and me. The number of services during Holy Week greatly increased his responsibilities and by Friday he was very tired. Yet the solemnity of the day seemed to give him renewed strength.

The most beautiful part of the day was the closing of the afternoon service when George sang, unaccompanied, the Reproaches.

"Oh my people, what have I come unto thee,
    or
Wherein have I wearied thee — Answer me
Because I brought thee forth from the land of
    Egypt
Thou hast prepared a cross for thy Saviour
Holy God
Holy Mighty
Holy and immortal, have mercy upon us."

Saturday — March 25

EVEN if I knew that tomorrow the world would go to pieces, I would still plant my apple tree.

— Martin Luther

SUNDAY — MARCH 26

Easter

"JESUS Christ is risen today. Hallelujah He is risen indeed. Hallelujah."

These words are the ancient greeting and response used by Christians to greet one another on Easter. Many churches have brought this greeting back into practice. It is usually followed by this glorious hymn:

Jesus Christ is risen today
Alleluia
Our triumphant holy day
Alleluia
Who died once upon the cross
Alleluia
Suffer to redeem our loss
Alleluia.

May the joy of Easter be with you today and always.

MONDAY — MARCH 27

A wise man once said "Live all the days of your life."

TUESDAY — MARCH 28

OUR Lord has written the promise of the Resurrection, not in books alone, but in every leaf in Springtime.

— *Martin Luther*

WEDNESDAY — MARCH 29

MY friend Marcia is one of a group of people sitting on the entrance committee of a Boston university and she often interviews prospective students. Over the years she has spoken with students from nearly every state in the U.S. but, as she writes in her letter, she has the most difficulty understanding the English of New York City applicants.

"A friend and I had some fun the other day doing definitions of certain 'strictly New York' pronunciations.

Oily: The opposite of late.

Sore: Viewed — I sore it in the store window.

Dare: Opposite of here — The dog is not here it is dare.

Use: A pronoun — Are use both going out?

Axe: To query — I want to axe you a question."

THE Spring comes slowly up this way,
Slowly, Slowly!
A little nearer every day.
— *Katherine Tynan Hinkson*

FORTY years ago on this date Newfoundland and Labrador became the tenth Canadian province. It is a magnificent part of our country and I, for one, am very happy to have this easternmost province as a part of our country of Canada.

April

WE ought to acquaint ourselves with the beautiful; we ought to contemplate it with rapture, and attempt to raise ourselves up to its height. And in order to gain strength from that, we must keep ourselves thoroughly unselfish — we must not make it our own, but rather seek to communicate it; indeed to make a sacrifice of it to those who are dear to us.

— *Goethe*

RECOMPENSE no man evil for evil.

— *Romans 12: 16*

Now that more spring-like weather is here I am most anxious to do more walking. I find walking to be an excellent exercise for me. I can set my own pace according to my energy level: a leisurely stroll when I am tired still gives me the needed exercise and a brisker pace makes me feel vital and energetic for the whole day.

The most important thing to remember if you are just starting to walk a great deal is that good footwear is essential. Most podiatrists recommend that you have each foot measured separately. Then buy for the longer foot, allowing at least one-half to one inch between the big toe and the tip of the shoe. A soft, pliable, but firm leather shoe is a good one for walking. It lets the foot "breathe." Shoes should be bought in the early afternoon (about the midpoint of your foot's expansion).

Happy hunting and welcome to the world of walking.

TUESDAY — APRIL 4

SEVERAL years ago a series of devastating tornadoes tore through the western city of Edmonton. Many people were killed and several hundred others were injured. Homes were levelled and many families lost all that they possessed in those nightmarish few minutes.

The people of Edmonton, and indeed all across Canada, were wonderful. Relief stations were set up to help the victims of the disaster. Families opened their homes to survivors. Large companies donated thousands of dollars to aid in rebuilding destroyed homes.

It was a time of numbing grief for hundreds of families and yet I'm sure that this time was made easier for them when they saw how much strangers cared.

WEDNESDAY — APRIL 5

I believe that when the soul disappears from this world, it disappears only to become manifest upon another scene in the wondrous drama of eternity.

— *Edwin Markham*

THE HERITAGE BOOK

M^Y brother Ben has a lovely old English bulldog who is adored by the neighbourhood children. She seldom barks and an intruder would risk death only from drowning in slobber.

Joya has only one quirk and that is that anything that comes through the mail slot in the front door is quickly disposed of by teeth shredding. The mailman therefore always rang the bell and personally delivered the mail into Ben or Marie's hands.

Last week there was a new unsuspecting letter carrier on their route. As he opened the slot to push in the letters they were ripped out of his hands and he could hear shredding and tearing noises.

The white-faced mailman looked at his hand as if to make sure that no part of it had been lost and with a very bewildered shake of his head he walked away muttering "I sure hope they don't get a *lot* of bills."

FRIDAY — APRIL 7

FRIENDS of Marg and Bruce have a large family who visit often. However, several weeks went by in this past winter when none of the children stopped in to visit.

On the weekend that they were all arriving Jane's husband admonished "Now don't go nagging the children—they've been very busy."

As the children arrived Jane didn't say a word. She simply handed each one a small sticky-backed piece of paper that said "HI, MY NAME IS — with a blank space to fill in the name.

SATURDAY — APRIL 8

NOSTALGIA is when you live life in the past lane.

SUNDAY — APRIL 9

I shall light a candle of understanding in thine heart, which shall not be put out.
— *The Apocrypha 10: 15*

THE HERITAGE BOOK

"THE more the merrier."
We are all familiar with expressions such as these that are used every day. I never knew just how old they were until I checked the sources of some of the more popular ones used in our family. I was astonished as I'm sure you will be too.

The more the merrier.
— Cicero (106-43 B.C.)

Let us let bygones be bygones.
— Epictetus (1st century A.D.)

The end justifies the means.
— Publilius Syrus (1st century B.C.)

While there is life there is hope.
— Cicero

Neither snow, nor rain, nor heat, nor gloom of night stays these couriers from the swift completion of their appointed rounds.
— Herodotus (484-424 B.C.)

Familiarity breeds contempt.
— Publilius Syrus

TUESDAY — APRIL 11

IF of thy mortal goods thou are bereft,
And from thy slender store two loaves
   alone to thee are left,
Sell one, and with the dole
   buy hyacinths to feed thy soul.
                    — *Gulistan of Moslih Edden Saadi*

WEDNESDAY — APRIL 12

IT is by presence of mind in untried emergen-
cies that the native metal of a man is tested.
                    — *James Russell Lowell*

THURSDAY — APRIL 13

PEOPLE are lonely because they build walls
instead of bridges.

THE HERITAGE BOOK

IN the past decade many large companies have offered early retirement to older executives in order to bring younger, dynamic men and women into their fold. In many cases this worked out well for all concerned but in others it did not. Although the younger people came with bright new ideas and plenty of enthusiasm they lacked one very important element — experience.

Some senior executives are now bringing back experienced people that had accepted early retirement.

My good friend John Burns is one of those people. John, who is now sixty-six, has returned to his former company as a consultant three days a week. As the company president recently told him, "I respect the young fresh ideas but now I know that nothing can substitute for experience."

THERE is not enough darkness in all the world to put out the light of one small candle.

SUNDAY — APRIL 16

WHEN I sit in darkness, the Lord shall be a light unto me.

— Micah 7: 8

MONDAY — APRIL 17

HOW many million Aprils came
Before I ever knew
How white a cherry bough could be,
A bed of squills, how blue!

— Sara Teasdale

As Marg and I walked today we saw the very beginnings of blossoms on some of the trees. How pleasant it is to see these early signs of spring and to know that soon our bare trees and gardens will be filled again with beautiful blooms.

TUESDAY — APRIL 18

LABOUR to keep alive in your breast that little spark of celestial fire — conscience.

— George Washington

THE HERITAGE BOOK

WHAT is this passing scene?
A peevish April day!
A little sun, a little rain,
And then night sweeps along the plain
And all things fade away.

— Henry Kirke White

IF your luck isn't what it should be, write a "p" in front of it and try again.

— Bob Edwards

IF you haven't time to help youngsters find the right way in life, somebody with more time will help them find the wrong way.

— T. Mack

OUR goal in life should be to make the world great enough to justify the wonder in a small child's eyes.

— B. Williams

So Jesus spoke again "In truth, in very truth I tell you, I am the door of the sheepfold. The sheep paid no heed to any who came before me, for they were all thieves and robbers. I am the door, anyone who comes into the fold through me shall be safe. He shall go in and out and find pasturage."

— John 10: 7–9

ANATOLE France once wrote "To know is nothing at all; to imagine is everything."

Many children today spend hours and hours watching T.V. or playing video games. Neither of these requires much thought or imagination.

If children don't spend time playing or making up fun things to do when they are young, the imagination will stagnate and they will become bored teenagers and adults.

Certainly television and computers have their place in society but let's not ruin our next generation — imagination *is* everything.

TUESDAY — APRIL 25

MY friend Jake Frampton often reads critics' reports on new books so that he is able to give customers several viewpoints on the book they are buying.

One of his favourite reviews was a one-sentence report that read, "Miss Black's new book is underwhelming."

WEDNESDAY — APRIL 26

THE signs of spring are all around us. As I walked through our neighbourhood today I saw robins in many trees.

Know you why the robin's breast
Gleameth of a dusky red,
Like the lustre 'mid the stars
Of the potent planet Mars?
'Tis — a monkish myth has said —
Owing to his cordial heart;
For, long since, he took the part
Of those hapless children, sent
Heavenward, for punishment;
And to quench the fierce desire
Bred in them by ruthless fire,
Brought on tiny bill and wing
Water from some earthly spring.
— *Paul Hamilton Hayne*

THURSDAY — APRIL 27

PEOPLE always laugh at the fool things you try to do until they discover that you are making money out of them.

— Bob Edwards

FRIDAY — APRIL 28

As I am well aware, one can never know everything there is to be known about human nature. One can be sure only of one thing, and that is that it will never cease to have a surprise in store for you.

— W. Somerset Maugham

SATURDAY — APRIL 29

THE worst bankrupt in the world is the man who has lost his enthusiasm. Let him lose everything but enthusiasm and he will come through again to success.

THE HERITAGE BOOK

T<small>HERE</small> are times when many of us have our doubts about the institutional Church. We wonder how effective it is in a contemporary society that has become one of violence and brutality, irresponsibility and falsehood.

Then in the midst of the cynicism that begins to take over our soul, we come upon some of the words of Christ.

"A new commandment I give unto you, that you love one another as I have loved you."

We remember that these words were spoken in a time of brutality and terror, when life was cheap and morality was at a new low. Still Christ had faith and hope for humanity.

If we believe Christ's commandment dare we stop trying and believing? I think not.

May

MONDAY — MAY 1

KIND hearts are the gardens,
Kind thoughts are the roots.
Kind words are the flowers,
Kind deeds are the fruits.

Take care of the gardens,
And keep them from weeds.
Fill, fill them with flowers,
Kind words and kind deeds.
— *Henry Wadsworth Longfellow*

TUESDAY — MAY 2

WE shall be made truly wise if we be made content; content, too not only with what we can understand, but content with what we do not understand — the habit of mind which theologians call, and rightly, faith in God.
— *Charles Kingsley*

THE HERITAGE BOOK

THIS morning as Marg and I were crawling along in Toronto-bound traffic I remembered another such morning several years ago. There had been a serious highway accident and a small boy had been terribly injured. The ambulance had arrived but the attendant was not optimistic.

"If we can get him to Sick Kids he has a chance, but with this traffic, well — "

There happened to be a young traffic reporter standing there listening.

"Let me try something. You guys be ready to go."

He called in to his station and asked them to broadcast an appeal to motorists to clear the passing lane to Toronto. The announcer then phoned the message to all other stations in the area. One by one they interrupted their broadcasts with the appeal.

The response was incredible. As the ambulance raced on to Toronto, siren wailing, the passing lane was cleared all the way to the hospital. Thanks to caring people, a small boy had been given a chance.

Thursday — May 4

IN walking, the will and the muscles are so accustomed to working together and performing their task with so little expenditure of force that the intellect is left comparatively free.

— Oliver Wendell Holmes

Friday — May 5

MAY is white clouds behind pine trees Puffed out and marching upon a blue sky.

— Amy Lowell

Saturday — May 6

COURAGE is what it takes to stand up and speak; courage is also what it takes to sit down and listen.

SUNDAY — MAY 7

I will not leave you desolate says the Lord. I will come to you.

— John 14: 18

During the period of expectancy between the Ascension and Pentecost (the gift of the Holy Spirit) we can find strength in Christ's promise.

MONDAY — MAY 8

JOHN Diefenbaker was a capital "C" Conservative. It was unusual therefore to see him welcome Gerald Regan, a Liberal, to the House of Commons.

"Although I don't usually welcome Liberals to the Commons in your case I will make an exception," said the smiling Mr. Diefenbaker. "I am glad to have you there — you speak worse French than I do!"

TUESDAY — MAY 9

ONE of the tragedies of life is the murder of a beautiful theory by a brutal gang of facts.

— Duc de la Rochefoucauld

WE all love a good loser if it isn't us.

MY granddaughter Phyllis's good friend Christie has been teaching a grade five class this year. Several of the children in the class have severe reading problems. They can only cope with a level of book much beneath their years. The children felt that reading "baby books" as they called them was demeaning until Christie had an inspiration.

"Mrs. Stewart's grade one needs story tellers for several groups in her class" she announced. "Each day I will be choosing certain students to read to them. Of course they will need stories that are interesting to grade ones."

Her idea has been a huge success. The younger children enjoy the stories and it has boosted the egos of the older children to have others in awe of their ability to read.

How lucky they are to have such a caring teacher.

FRIDAY — MAY 12

L IFE has loveliness to sell,
All beautiful and splendid things
Blue waves whitened on a cliff,
Soaring fire that sways and sings,
And children's faces looking up
Holding wonder like a cup.

Life has loveliness to sell,
Music like a curve of gold,
Scent of pine trees in the rain,
Eyes that love you, arms that hold
And for your spirit's still delight,
Holy thoughts that star the night.

Spend all you have for loveliness,
Buy it and never count the cost;
For one white singing hour of peace
Count many a year of strife well lost,
And for a breath of ecstasy
Give all you have been or could be.

— *Sara Teasdale*

SATURDAY — MAY 13

I T is very easy to forgive others their mistakes; it takes more grit and gumption to forgive them for having witnessed your own.

SUNDAY — MAY 14

Mother's Day

A s long ago we carried to your knees
   The tales and treasures of eventful days
Knowing no deed too humble for your praise,
Nor any gift too trivial to please,
So still we bring with older smiles and tears
What gifts we may to claim the old, dear right;
Your faith beyond the silence and the night;
Your love still close and watching through
   the years.

Our minister read us this lovely poem in church this morning. I found it a very fitting piece for all mothers.

MONDAY — MAY 15

I F a man does not make new acquaintances as he advances through life, he will soon find himself left alone. A man, sir, should keep his friendship in a constant repair.

— *Samuel Johnson*

THE HERITAGE BOOK

<u>TUESDAY — MAY 16</u>

My friends Will and Muriel Hampton stopped in for tea this afternoon. They were on their way home from a Red Cross blood donor clinic where both had donated blood.

Our hospital system in Canada depends on donated blood for all of its surgical needs. The blood is available, free of charge, because of the Red Cross and their clinics.

In the U.S. and many other countries people are paid for donating blood and the user must pay for it in turn.

Ours is a far better system and we should be grateful to the Red Cross volunteers who regularly donate their time to staff these clinics, so vital to our patient care.

<u>WEDNESDAY — MAY 17</u>

A house with daffodils in it is a house lit up, whether or no the sun be shining outside.
— *A.A. Milne*

THE HERITAGE BOOK

MY husband George and I used to go to the movies infrequently. It was not that we didn't enjoy movies, but our budget didn't allow a great many luxuries.

When we *did* go it was often to see a Jimmy Stewart film.

James Maitland Stewart got his first acting job the summer after he graduated from Princeton with a degree in architecture. He joined a summer stock company with his friend, Henry Fonda.

He went from bit parts on Broadway to star billing in Hollywood and yet wherever he worked he was thought of as "Mr. Nice Guy," an unusual term in the cutthroat movie business.

Of all the Jimmy Stewart movies my favourite remains *The Glenn Miller Story*.

Perhaps this comment best explains Jimmy Stewart's appeal.

"I like some of my pictures better than others. But I always tried, and if the script wasn't too good, well, then I just tried a little harder."

Friday — May 19

RICH people miss one of the greatest thrills in life — paying the last installment.

Saturday — May 20

SYDNEY J. Harris made a most interesting observation:

"Young people searching for their 'real self' must learn that the real self is not something one finds as much as it is something one makes; and it is one's daily actions that shape the inner personality far more permanently than any amount of introspection or intellection."

Sunday — May 21

O Father, my hope
O Son, my refuge
O Holy Spirit, my protection
Holy Trinity, glory to thee.
— *Comptine-Eastern Orthodox*

MONDAY — MAY 22

TODAY is Memorial Day in the United States. "What is so universal as death must be a benefit."

— Friedrich Schiller

TUESDAY — MAY 23

THIS past weekend was the Victoria Day holiday weekend. Here in Ontario it is often used to open cottages that have been closed up since the last Thanksgiving weekend.

On this holiday, Marg, Bruce, and I went north to Muskoka to help my friend Eleanor with this springtime ritual.

Eleanor's cottage is, in fact, an old Muskoka home built many years ago. Although it has had many improvements (new kitchen, full indoor bathroom) it still has its old rustic charm. There is a full screened porch running across the front for bug-free reading and, in very hot weather, sleeping.

Bruce attended to the outdoor chores while Marg, Eleanor, and I cleaned inside.

By Monday afternoon all was once again in order for another summer season.

Many hands do indeed make light work!

THE HERITAGE BOOK

ON this date in 1819 Princess Alexandrina Victoria was born in London, England. She was the daughter of Prince Edward, Duke of Kent and Princess Victoria.

On June 28, 1837, just one month after her eighteenth birthday, Victoria was crowned Queen of England. Her poise, modesty, and good sense made an immediately favourable impression on the nation. She increased her popularity by promptly paying her father's debts, which were considerable.

In 1840 Victoria married her twenty-year-old cousin, Prince Albert, who was largely responsible for setting the tone of moral earnestness and strait-laced propriety of the Victorian Era, as it became known.

Victoria's strength lay in her good common sense and directness of character. She was Britain's longest reigning monarch during a fascinating period in history.

THURSDAY — MAY 25

MARSHALL'S wife Jamie called this evening with a rather harrowing tale.

As she was preparing dinner, grease in a pan she was using caught fire. Fortunately she had a small fire extinguisher beside the stove and she was able to smother the fire very quickly.

The incident left her very shaken, however. Her call this evening was to make sure that both Marg and I had a good, easy-to-use extinguisher in our kitchens.

In fact neither of us do but my son-in-law Bruce plans to remedy that situation tomorrow.

The new extinguishers are very small and light and, according to the Fire Department, no household should be without one.

FRIDAY — MAY 26

THE ability to laugh together is the essence of love.

— *Francoise Sagan*

SATURDAY — MAY 27

G OD scatters love on every side
Freely among his children all,
And always hearts are lying open wide
Wherein some grains may fall.

— James Russell Lowell

SUNDAY — MAY 28

THE second half of the Christian calendar begins with this Sunday. During the first half from Advent to Trinity Sunday we have remembered the main events in the life of Christ here on earth. The Sundays after Pentecost are concerned with the practical life of those who believe in Christ. It is the season of growth in Christian living.

MONDAY — MAY 29

IT would do the world good if every man in it would compel himself occasionally to be absolutely alone. Most of the world's progress has come out of such loneliness.

— Bruce Barton

To Age

WELCOME, old friend. These many years
Have we lived door by door;
The Fates have laid aside their shears
Perhaps for some few more.

I was indocile at an age
When better boys were taught,
But thou at length hast made me sage,
If I am sage in aught.

Little I know from other men,
Too little they from me,
But thou hast pointed well the pen
That writes these lines to thee.

Thanks for expelling Fear and Hope,
One vile, the other vain;
One's scourge, the other's telescope,
I shall not see again!

Rather what lies before my feet
My notice shall engage —
He who hath braved Youth's dizzy heat
Dreads not the frost of Age.

— Walter Savage Landor

THE HERITAGE BOOK

I hear them say I am dying—
And I laugh.
I know I look to them like a dry and withered
  leaf
That has let go at last,
Fluttering to the ground to be forever buried.
I am alone in the purple shadow,
And over the dim hill in the twilight
Comes the tall White Elephant
And his rider, the Dark Prince!
They whisper, "It is the end!"
And I laugh —
For I know it is the beginning!

— Jewell Bothwell Tull

June

"LOVE is a short word but it contains everything. Love means the body, the soul, the life, the entire being. We feel love as we feel the warmth of our blood, we breathe love as we breathe the air, we hold it in ourselves as we hold our thoughts. Nothing more exists for us. Love is not a word; it is a wordless state indicated by four letters. . . ."

I write these lines about love by Guy de Maupassant as I remember our wedding day so many years ago. George and I were so very young then but we were very much in love.

Although George is no longer here I remember our life together with love.

THE HERITAGE BOOK

O NE of the more difficult aspects of being a
minister's child is dealing with peers who
usually assign them the role of "goody-goody."

Our daughters Mary and Marg dealt fairly
well with this problem. Julia had more difficulty. She felt compelled to prove that she
could be as "bad" as her friends. But fortunately her friends were a nice group of youngsters, so "bad" became a relative term. George
and I accepted her rebelliousness quite easily
— in fact I think George was secretly quite
pleased to see his daughter accepted as one of
the gang.

There was only one time that we really had
to lay down the law. Julia's friends had begun
to smoke, and suddenly Julia was lighting up
too.

George took Julia aside and spoke to her
quietly but firmly. "If you truly enjoy smoking
Julia then do it. You may not smoke in our
home but I won't forbid you to smoke else-
where," he said. "But if you are smoking to be
one of the gang I hope you will decide against
it."

From that day to this Julia never smoked
again.

SATURDAY — JUNE 3

MARG, Bruce, and I drove into the countryside today for a picnic lunch in a small park. On a riverbank nearby was the most beautiful lilac bush I think I have ever seen. It was tall but the blooms seemed to grow at all levels and not just on the top as often seems to happen.

As we sat and enjoyed the beautiful scent I was quite surprised to see a young couple arrive with shears and begin picking a large bouquet. The young man, seeing my frown of disapproval, came over to speak to us.

"My grandfather planted this bush years ago and he said that it would stay healthy only if the blooms were picked each year. We'd be happy to have you folks help yourselves as well."

I felt like a foolish old lady.

SUNDAY — JUNE 4

HOLY Father, cheer our way
With Thy love's perpetual ray;
Grant us every closing day
Light at evening time.
— *Hymn: Rev. B. H. Robinson*

Monday — June 5

Take a rest; a field that has rested gives a beautiful crop.

— *Ovid*

Tuesday — June 6

Dr. Albert Schweitzer was asked how parents could best pass on to their children the proper attitude toward responsibility. His reply was "There are three ways: 1) Example 2) Example 3) Example."

Wednesday — June 7

Great it is to believe the dream
When we stand in youth by the starry stream;
But a greater thing is to fight life thru
And say at the end "The dream is true."

Thursday — June 8

Faith is the daring of the soul to go farther than it can see.

— *William Newton Clark*

Friday — June 9

M Y birthday seems to have crept up on me when I wasn't watching. So it was with unfeigned surprise this evening that I greeted many members of our large family as they gathered to celebrate the occasion.

We were lucky to have a fine warm evening and our outdoor potluck supper was a great success.

The highlight of the dinner was a white cake that the newest member of our family had made. Marshall's wife Jamie Ann must have spent hours of her time fashioning this cake. It had somehow been shaped like a vase containing a bouquet of lilies. The flowers and the leaves were done with coloured icing and the whole effect was magnificent.

I felt very honoured that Jamie would take so much time to give us such pleasure.

Saturday — June 10

C ONSCIENCE is God's presence in man.

THE HERITAGE BOOK

O God, I was as glad of thy Word
As a man who knows all about pearls
coming across one of priceless beauty.
So perfect that he cannot be happy unless he
possesses it;
So he sells all that he has and with eager joy
buys that pearl.
O God, I am glad, unspeakably glad, for thy
word and thy kingdom.

AND what is so rare as a day in June?
Then, if ever come perfect days;
Then Heaven tries earth if it be in tune,
And over it softly her warm ear lays.
— *James Russell Lowell*

THERE is the greatest practical benefit in
making a few failures early in life.
— *Thomas Henry Huxley*

THE HERITAGE BOOK

MARY McConnell stopped in for tea this afternoon. During our chat she mentioned that her younger children wanted to go to summer camp.

Remembering my own summers at camp I said I was sure they would enjoy the outdoor experience. Her reply surprised me.

"If it were camp as you know it I'd be happy, Edna, but Jeff wants to go to 'hockey camp' and John insists that *everyone* is going to 'computer camp'. I don't really want them in an arena or in front of a T.V. screen during the short months of good weather. I hope they will understand our reasons for saying 'no.'"

I hope so too.

THE ideal man bears the accidents of life with dignity and grace, making the best of circumstances.

— *Aristotle*

THE responsibility of tolerance lies with those who have wider vision.

— *George Eliot*

THE HERITAGE BOOK

I must confess that when it comes to using the metric system for cooking and baking I am quite hopeless.

I have so many wonderful recipes that came to me from my mother and grandmother that I would like to pass on to my grandchildren. But when I try to convert these to metric measure the results are usually disastrous.

I know that metric is here to stay so one day soon I guess I'll have to accept it. Not today, though.

I think that one of the finest tributes any man can receive is to hear his children say "He's a good father."

I can say without reservation that my own dad was a wonderful father. I miss him on this Father's Day and yet I know how lucky I was to be his daughter.

"A Father is a priceless treasure."

MONDAY — JUNE 19

STEPHEN Leacock was once invited to accompany a group of bird watchers on a pre-dawn expedition.

Mr. Leacock answered the invitation in his own inimitable style.

"Ladies, I regret to tell you that I am the kind of man who would have absolutely no interest in an oriole building a nest unless it built it in my hat in the check room at my club."

TUESDAY — JUNE 20

I have always enjoyed ballet so when Jake Frampton told me this little anecdote this evening I found it very amusing.

Several years ago the "Sleeping Beauty" ballet was being taped for television. The cameraman assigned usually covered sports programs, and so the producer offered this suggestion. "Just pretend that this is a hockey game and Rudolf Nureyev is the puck."

WEDNESDAY — JUNE 21

CHARACTER is like the foundation of a house — it is below the surface.

Thursday — June 22

Summer has arrived again and I welcome it with open arms. I love the weather, I love the beauty of the flowers but more than these, I love the long days.

Mrs. McGuiness and I sat out in the garden enjoying the evening light. It is almost as if the sun is reluctant to leave for even a few hours.

As we sat and watched the stars come out I rejoiced at the arrival of summer in my small corner of the universe.

Friday — June 23

O world, I cannot hold thee close enough!
— *Edna St. Vincent Millay*

Saturday — June 24

This is St. Jean Baptiste Day, a very special day for French Canadians.

In the province of Quebec this day is celebrated with unbridled enthusiasm.

If you are of French Canadian heritage I wish you a happy St. Jean Baptiste Day.

THE HERITAGE BOOK

THIS nun's prayer for the seventeenth century is pertinent for all of us as we grow older.

"Lord, thou knowest better than I know myself that I am growing older and will someday be old. Release me from craving to straighten out everyone's affairs. With my vast store of wisdom, it seems a shame not to use it all, but thou knowest, Lord, that I want a few friends at the end.

"Give me the ability to see good things in unexpected places and in unexpected people. And give me Lord, the grace to tell them so. Amen."

DO not lose your desire to walk; every day I walk myself into a state of well-being and walk away from every illness; I have walked myself into my best thoughts, and I know of no thought so burdensome that one cannot walk away from it.

— *Sören Kierkegaard*

THE HERITAGE BOOK

My good friend Lillian lives in a nursing home. In the afternoon she and several other residents often play bridge. The games are taken quite seriously.

Lillian recounted, in a recent letter, that she and her partner bid seven hearts, vulnerable. After several minutes of deliberation her opponent took out a nitroglycerin tablet, slipped it under her tongue and with a resigned sigh said "I double."

The more you love, the more you'll find
That life is good and friends are kind
For only what we give away
Enriches us from day to day
— *Helen Steiner Rice*

God gave man an upright countenance to survey the heavens, and to look upward to the stars.

THE HERITAGE BOOK

My good friend Betty has been bedridden for a number of years. Many people in her condition might have been bitter — not Betty. Her sunny, cheerful disposition has made her a good friend to many and an inspiration to other disabled people.

Betty's attitude, long a source of amazement to her doctors, is soon going to be a resource of hope to others with similar afflictions.

Betty has made a tape, with the doctors, discussing her illness, how she has dealt with it, and how she lives happily with acceptance of her condition. She hopes that it may give someone else the patience and endurance to go on in life and to be happy once again.

It is this unselfish giving of herself that makes Betty an inspiration to all of us. I admire her greatly.

July

I believe that "The Athenian Oath" offers one of the most positive outlooks for citizens of any country. It is particularly appropriate on this Canada Day.

"We will never bring disgrace to this, our nation, by any act of dishonesty or cowardice, nor ever desert our suffering comrades in the ranks. We will fight for the ideals of the nation both alone and with others. We will revere and respect our nation's laws, and do our best to incite a like respect and reverence in those above us who are prone to annul and set them at naught. We will strive unceasingly to quicken the public's sense of civic duty. Thus in all these ways we will transmit this nation not only not less but greater, better, and more beautiful than it was transmitted to us."

THE HERITAGE BOOK

GOD who didst lead the fathers of our nation into this land of Canada and has increased us by thy favour, grant we who beseech thee, that we who now enter into their inheritance may prove ourselves a people mindful of thy mercies and ready to do thy will, through Jesus Christ our Lord. Amen.

GOALS are like stars; they may not be reached, but they can always be a guide.

THIS is the day when our neighbours to the south celebrate Independence Day.

Americans are unabashedly, unapologetically proud of being American. And they're very vocal about it.

America began a couple of hundred years ago, with nothing but a few immigrants who were, generally, poor and uneducated. In this short time they tamed a wilderness and turned it into the most powerful nation on earth. Is it any wonder they shout it from the rooftops?

THE HERITAGE BOOK

M Y son-in-law Bruce is an avid golfer. He will often stop off after work and play a few holes before going home to dinner.

Bruce was home earlier than usual today. He also seemed rather subdued so Marg asked, "Didn't you play golf today dear?"

"Yes."

"Is there something wrong?"

Suddenly he grinned and gave a shout that nearly sent Marg off her chair. "I did it! I got a hole in one!"

By this time he was fairly dancing around the room.

"It was on the third hole. I shot it straight from the tee into the cup. I couldn't believe my eyes."

Bruce is justifiably proud of this. Many golfers never get a hole in one in a lifetime of golfing.

THURSDAY — JULY 6

T ACT is the unsaid part of what you think.

Friday — July 7

It takes tough seas to make good sailors and great captains.

Saturday — July 8

I enjoyed a lovely day with Marshall and Jamie today. The heat wave of the past few days has kept me pretty much indoors so I was delighted when Marshall called and suggested an outing to Niagara-on-the-Lake.

We stopped at the Niagara School of Horticulture and toured their magnificent gardens. I was very impressed. The young men and women are being trained so that they may take their skills throughout Ontario to make beautiful parks and recreational areas.

It was easy to see that their training is excellent. The gardens are beautifully laid out and the quality of blooms is unrivalled. I hope that I may visit these gardens again.

BE of good cheer; I have overcome the world.

— John 16: 33

BACK in July of 1987 we were having a heat wave of record proportions.

On Sunday morning the minister rose to give his sermon. His face was flushed and dripping perspiration. As he wiped his face he said to those few of us in the congregation:

"It seems to me that if this heat doesn't make you reflect on your sins, nothing I can say will."

End of sermon.

IT is never too late to give up your prejudices.

HENRY David Thoreau, on music: "When I hear music I fear no danger, I am invulnerable, I see no foe. I am related to the earliest times and to the latest."

THURSDAY — JULY 13

WE say: Don't blame others for your own mistakes.

The Spanish say: One does not see one's own faults but only those of one's neighbours.

The Koreans say: Blame yourself and not the stream if you fall in the water.

FRIDAY — JULY 14

As I sat on the patio this afternoon I had an amazing experience.

I was reading quietly in my chair when I became conscious of a whirring noise. I looked up and saw a tiny hummingbird feeding on our hanging planters. I stayed very still as it moved from flower to flower sucking the nectar into its needle-like beak.

Suddenly it looked over and realized that I was there. Instead of flying away it came right over in front of my face. Its tiny wings were buzzing and it hovered beak to nose, as it were. It remained there, staring at me, for about ten seconds and then it flew swiftly away.

SATURDAY — JULY 15

MY grandson Fred called today. Young Geoffrey has picked up a bug and is feeling somewhat under the weather.

June took him to the doctor, who prescribed medication to be taken for ten days.

"The funniest part," said Fred, "is that it is to be taken one hour before or two hours after eating. As June has pointed out, there never *is* one hour before or two hours after this boy eats."

SUNDAY — JULY 16

BLESS the Lord, my soul; my innermost heart, bless his holy name.
Bless the Lord, my soul and forget not all his benefits.

— Psalm 103

MONDAY — JULY 17

A kind word picks up a man when trouble weighs him down.

THE HERITAGE BOOK

I heard an American interviewed on the radio today and his accent brought to mind an amusing incident of several years ago.

A good friend of mine, Jim Dundas, was in hospital in Buffalo, New York. He suffered from emphysema and was on a respirator in the intensive care unit.

His wife Beverly and I sat throughout the day in the small waiting room with relatives of the other I.C.U. patients. One of the other people waiting said that her husband had just been taken off the respirator.

"He was so happy," she exclaimed "to be allowed salads again."

I thought this a little unusual but said nothing. Finally I asked "Isn't that a bit unusual — giving a salad to someone who has had nothing but liquid through a tube for two weeks?"

She looked at me oddly and then laughed heartily. With her Buffalo accent I mistook "solid" for "salad."

WEDNESDAY — JULY 19

MARCUS Tullius Cicero wrote "In Praise of Literature" in the first century B.C. It is relevant even today.

"But this gives stimulus to our youth and diversion to our old age; this adds a charm to success, and offers a haven of consolation to failure. In the home it delights, in the world it hampers not. Through the night-watches, on all our journeying, and in our hours of country ease, it is an unfailing companion."

THURSDAY — JULY 20

SOME people see more in a walk around the block than others see in a trip around the world.

FRIDAY — JULY 21

OUR church magazine had an amusing cartoon this month.

An usher is shown passing a collection plate at a church wedding. The caption reads "I admit sir that it's very unusual — but the bride's father insisted."

THE HERITAGE BOOK

I am spending some time with my friend Eleanor in Muskoka this week.

Our days together are very comfortable. We rise early and have a cup of tea on the porch before eating our breakfast. After breakfast we usually take a long walk. In the afternoon we often read out on the dock, and if the day is warm we cool off with quick dips in the lake. After a late dinner we watch the stars come out.

One of the finest things about friendship is that we can have companionable silence as well as good conversation.

PRAISE my soul the king of Heaven
To his feet thy tributes bring;
Ransomed, healed, restored, forgiven
Who like thee his praise shall sing?
Praise him, praise him, alleluia
Praise the everlasting King.

— *Henry Francis Lyte*

MONDAY — JULY 24

ELEANOR gave me this poem for today. It is actually a prayer found in Chester Cathedral, England.

Give me a good digestion, Lord,
And also something to digest;
Give me a healthy body, Lord.
With sense to keep it at its best.

Give me a healthy mind, Lord,
To keep the good and pure in sight;
Which, seeing sin, is not appalled,
But finds a way to set it right.

Give me a mind that is not bored
That does not whimper, whine or sigh;
Don't let me worry overmuch,
About the fussy thing called "I."

Give me a sense of humour, Lord,
Give me the grace to see a joke;
To get some happiness from life,
And pass it on to other folk.

TUESDAY — JULY 25

THOMAS Fuller, an English historian and clergyman, wrote that "accusing the times is but excusing ourselves." It is relevant today in spite having been written over three hundred years ago.

WEDNESDAY — JULY 26

THE weather today was so hot that we spent much of the day in the cool of the porch.

The children next door spent all their time waterskiing, swimming, and diving off the dock. They were still swimming as Eleanor and I enjoyed our late dinner. Suddenly Michael, who is fifteen, shouted in alarm. "We need a doctor! Quick somebody!"

Young Chris, a pretty thirteen-year-old girl, was in the water with her entire face covered in blood. Her mother held a towel to her face as she and her husband pulled Chris from the lake.

Apparently Chris had slipped and dove too deeply, arriving face first on a rock.

A fast trip to the Bracebridge hospital revealed that Chris had a concussion, a broken nose, a severe laceration under the eye plus a scrape on the whole right side of her face.

But as the nurse at the hospital put it, "Most diving accidents don't walk in here."

THE HERITAGE BOOK

THURSDAY — JULY 27

Poor Chris is a sorry sight today. Her face is swollen and her eyes are blackened and shut. The bandage on her nose is enormous and she looks just terrible.

Her parents, although naturally upset, know that the consequences could have been much greater.

They have been in touch with a plastic surgeon in Toronto who had already spoken with the doctor in Bracebridge. He was most reassuring.

"Although she will look pretty terrible for some time to come I can assure you that she will look like herself again. There is nothing in her injuries that we won't be able to put right."

All of us were much relieved to hear his assurances, not least of all Chris, who, after a look in the mirror pronounced herself "Ugh — yucky!"

FRIDAY — JULY 28

A man who moves a mountain begins by carrying away small stones.

— *Chinese Proverb*

THE HERITAGE BOOK

WHO drives the horses of the sun
Shall lord it but a day;
Better the lowly deed were done,
And kept the humble way.

The rust will find the sword of fame,
The dust will hide the crown;
Aye, none shall nail so high his name
Time will not tear it down.

The happiest heart that ever beat
Was in some quiet breast
That found the common daylight sweet,
And left to Heaven the rest.

BEHOLD us, Lord, a little space
From daily tasks set free,
And met within thy holy place
To rest awhile with Thee.

— *Rev. John Ellerton*

IDLENESS is only the refuge of weak minds.

August

For those of you who enjoy an evening walk in the garden, I give you "Eventide" by Caroline Atherton Briggs Mason.

At cool of day with God I walk
My garden's grateful shade;
I hear His voice among the trees,
And I am not afraid.

He speaks to me in every wind,
He smiles from every star;
He is not deaf to me, nor blind,
Nor absent, nor afar.

His hand that shuts the flowers to sleep
Each in its dewy fold,
Is strong my feeble life to keep,
And competent to hold.

The powers below and the powers above,
Are subject to his care —
I cannot wander from His love
Who loves me everywhere.

Thus dowered, and guarded thus, with Him
I walk this peaceful shade;
I hear his voice among the trees,
And I am not afraid.

THE HERITAGE BOOK

ALTHOUGH I love to travel, I enjoy coming home. There is something very comforting in the feel and smell of one's own sheets in bed at night. There is warmth in the familiar things around us, pictures of our family, our beloved books.

East or west, home is best.

> — *Proverb, Bohn*

Such is the patriot's boast, where'er we roam, his first, best country ever is, at home.

> — *Oliver Goldsmith*

Peace and rest at length have come
All the day's long toil is past,
And each heart is whispering
"Home, home at last."

> — *Thomas Hood*

The midnight train is slow and old,
But of it let this thing be told,
To its high honour be it said,
It carries people home to bed.

> — *Joyce Kilmer*

Thursday — August 3

Cold words freeze people, and hot words scorch them; bitter words make them bitter and wrathful words make them wrathful. Kind words also produce their own image on men's souls, and a beautiful image it is. They smoothe and quiet, and comfort the hearer.

— *Blaise Pascal*

Friday — August 4

On this day ninety years ago the Queen Mother was born. She was loved and revered by all her subjects. This little anecdote will give you some idea why this dear lady is held in such esteem.

At a low point in the war for the Allies it was suggested that the two young princesses and their mother might leave England for a safer refuge.

The Queen Mother replied "The children will not leave unless I do. I shall not leave unless the King does, and the King will not leave the country in any circumstances whatever."

SATURDAY — AUGUST 5

I was interested to read about a program that trains dogs to assist the handicapped.

"Dogs for the Deaf" rescues abandoned dogs from shelters and trains them to respond to the needs of deaf people. The dogs hear a noise, touch the deaf person with a paw, and lead them to the sound. These animals can be trained to respond to smoke alarms, baby cries, doorbells, oven buzzers, and a host of other noises.

"Hearing Ear Dogs" are allowed the same public access as Seeing Eye Dogs and they are easily recognizable by their blaze-orange collars and leashes.

What a wonderful idea!

SUNDAY — AUGUST 6

O Lord, it is a good thing to give thee thanks, to sing Psalms to thy name, O Lord most High, to declare thy love in the morning and thy constancy every night.

— Psalm 92

MONDAY — AUGUST 7

MARG and Bruce have been working in the garden all evening and what a bountiful harvest they have brought in.

There is a basket of yellow beans, a collander of green peas and next to these a box of "sweet 100" tomatoes. These tomatoes grow in bunches like grapes and each bunch has at least ten small tomatoes. In the sink is chard waiting to be washed and Marg is putting away a freezer bag of snow peas.

Tomorrow Bruce and Marg plan to take much of this harvest to friends who now live in apartments and who miss their gardens.

TUESDAY — AUGUST 8

NEVER lose an opportunity of seeing anything that is beautiful; for beauty is God's handwriting—a wayside sacrament. Welcome it in every fair face, in every fair sky, in every fair flower, and thank God for it as a cup of blessing.

— *Ralph Waldo Emerson*

THE HERITAGE BOOK

An old friend from the Maritimes sent me a most interesting letter from California. She was staying at a beautiful California college and participating in a program known as "Elderhostel." It sounds fascinating.

"Elderhostel" is a program for senior citizens offered by many colleges all over North America. The courses include archeology, computers, and jazz, to name just a few. The participants live on campus for periods of one, two, or sometimes three weeks. The courses are very reasonable as is the accommodation.

Lillian wrote, "Edna, I have made many new friends and have learned how to operate a computer. This has been a wonderful experience and I only wish I had heard about it earlier."

Faith is not belief without proof, but trust without reservations.

FRIDAY — AUGUST 11

WE all have our own ideas of what love is but I think this poem encompasses almost all of them.

Love is —
Slow to suspect — quick to trust,

Slow to condemn — quick to justify,
Slow to offend — quick to defend,

Slow to belittle — quick to appreciate,
Slow to demand — quick to give,

Slow to provoke — quick to help,
Slow to resent — quick to forgive.

SATURDAY — AUGUST 12

NEVER fear shadows. They simply mean there's a light shining somewhere nearby.

SUNDAY — AUGUST 13

O God thou hast taught me from boyhood, all my life I have proclaimed thy marvellous works and now that I am old and my hairs are grey, forsake me not O God.

— Psalm 71: 17–18

THE HERITAGE BOOK

When Newfoundland and Labrador became Canada's newest province in 1949, it brought with it North America's oldest history. Even the intrepid explorers like Columbus, Cabot, and Cartier were five hundred years behind the first European settlers in Newfoundland.

Recently archeologists have authenticated the grave site of an Indian youth buried nearly nine thousand years ago at L'Anse Amour.

Newfoundland abounds with historic sites in every region. Just a few of these are the site of the first court of justice in North America at Trinity in 1615, the site of the first landing of the successful transatlantic telegraph cable at Heart's Content in 1866, and the site of the departure of the first transatlantic airplane flight by Alcock and Brown in 1919.

Of course the most interesting part of any visit to Newfoundland is the time spent with the people. They are friendly, hospitable, hard working, fun-loving and kindly.

It is a part of our country that is well worth visiting.

Tuesday — August 15

When things go wrong as they sometimes
will,
When the road you're trudging seems all up-
hill,
When the funds are low and the debts are
high,
And you want to smile but you have to sigh,
When care is pressing you down a bit —
Rest if you must but don't you quit!

Success is failure turned inside out,
The silver tint of the clouds of doubt
And you never can tell how close you are
It may be near when it seems afar.
So stick to the fight when you're hardest hit —
It's when things go wrong that you mustn't
quit.

Wednesday — August 16

He is rich who owns the day, and no one
owns the day who allows it to be invaded
by worry, fret and anxiety.

— *Ralph Waldo Emerson*

Thursday — August 17

Sorrow looks back, worry looks around,
faith looks up.

THE HERITAGE BOOK

I spent a most interesting day today with Phyllis, Bill, and the twins. We took a picnic lunch and paid a visit to the Halton County Radial Railway Museum.

This museum is a full-size, operating electric railway with train rides on a scenic mile of track through rural Ontario. The station has been restored to the turn of the century style. Jenny and Justin were fascinated by the stationmaster with his blue and gold uniform and his gold watch and chain.

They were equally intrigued by the old streetcar that took us on our tour. This car had serviced downtown Toronto some sixty years ago. For Phyllis, Bill, and the twins it was a new and novel experience. For me it was a ride that brought back many memories. George and I often used to ride streetcars during those lean years when we couldn't afford a car.

After our tour we ate our lunch in a very pretty picnic grove near the tracks.

It was a splendid way to pass a summer day.

SATURDAY — AUGUST 19

I have more memories than if I were a thousand years old.

— *Charles Baudelaire*

SUNDAY — AUGUST 20

THIS prayer of Manoah* is often used for expectant parents and grandparents. Manoah prayed to the Lord "If it please thee O Lord let the man of God whom thou didst send come again to tell us what we are to do with the boy who is to be born."

— *Book of Judges 13: 8*

*Manoah was the father of Samson who served for twenty years as a judge over Israel.

THE HERITAGE BOOK

SLEEP my love and peace attend thee,
All through the night;
Guardian angels God will lend thee,
All through the night;
Soft the drowsy hours are creeping,
Hill and dale in slumber steeping,
Love alone his watch is keeping —
All through the night.

PEGGY Cay, my good friend in England, lives in a small cottage that she has kept up on her own since her husband's passing many years ago. It is hard work but Peggy has done a good job until a recent illness laid her up for several months.

Word of Peggy's illness passed round her parish. The people decided to help out by painting her fences, weeding her garden, and repainting the entire interior of her small home.

During this time Peggy had been staying with friends. She was moved to tears when her friends brought her to her "new" home.

THE HERITAGE BOOK

MY good friend Mary McConnell stopped in today and we had a very interesting discussion about the difficulty of raising teenagers. Mary was particularly upset with one of her sons who had come in late and had neglected to phone.

"You know, Edna, I was happy to see him but I had been so worried that it was only my anger that showed. I shouted quite loudly about his inconsideration. He felt very badly and, after my tirade, so did I."

As we talked I remembered a booklet designed to explain parents to teenagers. It begins with a translation of parents' comments.

For example, if a parent says "This is a fine time to be getting home" it means "I've been worried about you. When you don't let me know you'll be late, I sit here imagining all sorts of awful things happening to you."

Raising teenagers isn't easy but Mary and her husband are doing a very fine job.

THURSDAY — AUGUST 24

GOD bless whoever invented sleep, the mantle that embraces the thoughts of all men, food that satisfies all hunger, the weight that balances the scales and makes the shepherd the same as the king, the fool the same as the wise man.

— Miguel de Cervantes

FRIDAY — AUGUST 25

HISTORIAN Thomas Balington Macaulay wrote in 1825:

"Many politicians of our time are in the habit of laying down as self evident the proposition that no people ought to be free until they are fit to use their freedom. The maxim is worthy of the fool in the old story, who had resolved not to go in the water until he had learned to swim. If men wait for liberty until they become wise and good in slavery, they may indeed wait forever."

SATURDAY — AUGUST 26

ANYONE who's ever stood on principle knows that it's a very lonely place to stand.

SUNDAY — AUGUST 27

FOR the beauty of the earth
For the glories of the skies
For the love which from our birth
Over and around us lies,
Lord of all to thee we raise
This our sacrifice of praise.

— Folliet Pierpont

MONDAY — AUGUST 28

COUNT your garden by the flowers
Never by the leaves that fall;
Count your days by golden hours
Don't remember clouds at all.

Count the nights by stars not shadows,
Count your life by smiles not tears,
And with joy on every birthday
Count your age by friends not years.

TUESDAY — AUGUST 29

THE tests of life are not made to break us. Trouble may demolish a man's business — but build up his character. The blow at the outward man may be the greatest blessing to the inner man. Adversity does not break men; it makes them.

— *Alfred A. Montepart*

WEDNESDAY — AUGUST 30

I am sure that if people had to choose between living where the noise of children never stopped and where it was never heard, all the good-natured and sound people would prefer the incessant noise to the incessant silence.

— *George Bernard Shaw*

THURSDAY — AUGUST 31

As the month of August draws to a close I can't help but have mixed feelings. I don't like to think that our summer season is nearly over but I will be glad to have all our neighbourhood children home from camps or cottages. It has been so quiet these last few weeks that I have felt rather lonely at times.

September

SEPTEMBER has always been a month that I enjoy. The heavy heat of the summer is past but the chill of autumn has not yet arrived. The flower gardens are at their most beautiful and the vegetables are also beginning to peak.

When the girls were younger it was the month that they returned to school and I regained the freedom that I had given up in the summer months.

When my husband George was alive it was a month that we tried to spend together. We often left the girls with our parents for a weekend or two and went away to renew old ties with friends long unseen.

Now it is a month when I have good friends come to visit and I replenish memories to last me through the long winter to come.

SATURDAY — SEPTEMBER 2

FOR the man sound in body and serene in mind there is no such thing as bad weather; every sky has its beauty, the storms which whip the blood do but make it pulse more vigorously.

— *George Gissing*

SUNDAY — SEPTEMBER 3

JESUS stood up to read the lesson and was handed the scroll of the prophet Isaiah. He opened the scroll and found the passage which says "The spirit of the Lord is upon me because he hast anointed me; He has sent me to announce good news to the poor, to proclaim release for prisoners and recovery of sight to the blind, to let the broken victims go free, to proclaim the year of the Lord's favour."

THE HERITAGE BOOK

TODAY is Labour Day, the final holiday of our summer season.

Labour Day was first celebrated by the Knights of Labour in New York City in 1882 and again in 1884. It is now a legal holiday in both the United States and Canada.

When I think of the term "labour" I like to remember people who are happy in their jobs. I think of the check-out girl who is never without a smile for her customers. I think of the garbageman who sings opera music all the way around town on his collections. Most of all I remember my husband George who loved every minute of his "labour" in God's service.

TODAY is the birthday of James Neal McDowell the fourth. Jim is the son of an old friend of mine, Neal McDowell, who passed away several years ago of cancer.

Jimmy and his wife Barb have two lovely children. They are a very happy family, active in the community and church.

I know Neal would be thrilled to see how well his son is carrying on his life within the boundaries of family love.

THE HERITAGE BOOK

WHAT a busy community ours is this week. The classrooms are filled with eager (and not so eager) young people. Parents are busy providing transportation for youngsters who have registered in various fall activities. The volunteer leaders of these groups are once again giving up many afternoons and evenings to provide special times for so many.

During this week our community college calendar arrived, showing the numerous courses available to people of all ages.

Marg has registered to continue with the Conversational French that she started last year and Bruce has been trying to talk me into taking a word processor course. In fact I have decided to continue to study music and hope that I may continue to improve.

It is hard to believe that the quiet days of summer have passed so quickly. I know that I will enjoy the busier times of autumn but I'll miss the days of leisure.

THURSDAY — SEPTEMBER 7

THE oldest, shortest words — "yes" and "no" — are those which require the most thought.

— *Pythagorus*

FRIDAY — SEPTEMBER 8

"SUCCESS in marriage is more than finding the right person; it's being the right person."

How true that statement is! At a time when divorce and family break-up is becoming more prevalent in our society it is important to remember that both partners in marriage must work hard to make it successful.

The temptation to lay the blame for problems on someone other than oneself is great. It is essential that both partners make every effort to be the best that they can, both for themselves and for their spouse.

Being the right person isn't easy but it is certainly worth every bit of your effort.

THE HERITAGE BOOK

IT is better to burn the candle at both ends, and in the middle too, than to put it away in the closet and let the mice eat it.

— *Henry Van Dyke*

LORD, who hast taught us that all our doings without love are nothing worth: Send thy Holy Spirit and pour into our hearts that most excellent gift of love, the very bond of peace and of all virtues, without which whosoever liveth is counted dead before thee; Grant this for thine only Son, Jesus Christ's, sake. Amen.

— *Book of Common Prayer*

THE highest compliment one person can bestow on another is to ask for advice.

TUESDAY — SEPTEMBER 12

I enjoyed this story told to me by my son-in-law, John.

A young man had just started in the ministry at his first parish. He and his young wife were visiting his parents' home for dinner on a Saturday evening. As the time approached for them to leave his wife seemed to be somewhat upset. Finally as they were leaving she was heard to say, "All right, if you want to go by the church you can practise baptising me just one more time. But I want you to know that you may *not* practise on me for your first funeral."

WEDNESDAY — SEPTEMBER 13

I T takes two to speak the truth — one to speak it and another to hear.
— *Henry David Thoreau*

THE HERITAGE BOOK

I find it interesting to hear how various towns and cities in this great country came to get their names. When Jake Frampton came by for tea this afternoon he had this story that I think you will find amusing.

In the 1800s a settler from Scotland, Sandy Grant, chose British Columbia as his new home. Some time after he arrived a friend took him out to view the surrounding area. He was amazed by the enormity of everything — Shuswap Lake, the trees, the mountains. His friend then pointed out a moose standing in the forest. The only moose that Sandy Grant had ever heard of was the moose that Robbie Burns wrote about in the lines:

Since ye hae mice as big as that
I wouldna like tae meet a rat —
And it maun be a good-sized cat
Would dare to tackle sic a moose

which he quoted to his friend.

The story spread and the other settlers had a good laugh. As the settlement grew it was decided that it should be named Sicamous and it remains this day as a thriving town in the westernmost province.

THE HERITAGE BOOK

To be content, look backward on those who possess less than yourself, not forward on those who possess more. If this does not make you content, you don't deserve to be happy.

— *Benjamin Franklin*

CHARACTER is built out of circumstances. From exactly the same material one man builds palaces, while another builds hovels.

— *G. H. Lewes*

O depth of wealth, wisdom, and knowledge in God! How unsearchable his judgements, how untraceable his ways. Who knows the mind of the Lord? Who has been his counsellor? Who has ever made a gift to him to receive a gift in return? Source, Guide, and Goal, of all that is — to Him be glory forever. Amen.

— *Romans 11: 33–36*

Monday — September 18

Lao-tse (ca. 565 B.C.) wrote these interesting views on leadership that are pertinent even today.

"A leader is best when people barely know he exists. Not so good when people obey and acclaim him. Worse when they despise him. But of a good leader who talks little when his work is done and his aim fulfilled, they will say: 'We did it ourselves.'"

Tuesday — September 19

Blue to the north is a sky so clear
It means the corner of the year
Has been turned, from now on all
Leaves and men face to the Fall.
                — *Robert P. Tristam Coffin*

Wednesday — September 20

When love and skill work together expect a masterpiece.

THE HERITAGE BOOK

I watched as two young girls left for the arena this afternoon carrying their hockey equipment. Christy and Jamie are neighbours and they have played for our local girls' hockey team for several years now.

When the girls first played it was for a house league novice boys' team. I remember very well their first game.

As they went into the dressing room before the game several of their male team-mates made comments. "Why do we have yucky girls on the team?" "How come we get girls and the Blue team doesn't?" The little girls said nothing. Jamie who was very shy was near to tears.

But much to the boys' surprise the girls were excellent skaters and dominant factors in the game. The final score was a 7-1 win with Christy scoring four goals and Jamie three.

On the way off the ice the opposing team was taunted with cries of "Too bad you don't have girls on your team!"

FRIDAY — SEPTEMBER 22

MUHAMMED Ali, the famous boxer, was always well known for his enormous ego. A fine demonstration of this was a remark that he once made about his choice of careers.

"I once thought about playing football. But you have to wear too much equipment and people can't see you."

SATURDAY — SEPTEMBER 23

MY friend Marcia, who lives in Boston, sent me this amusing anecdote in a letter.

The superintendent of the Boston Public Library system was visiting a branch where an elderly gentleman had just signed out a large number of detective stories. The supervisor mentioned to one of the librarians that perhaps she could improve the man's literary taste by suggesting a book, other than a mystery, that he could read on occasion.

The librarian replied "I had thought of doing that until I found out who he is. That gentleman is the president of Harvard University."

THE HERITAGE BOOK

THEREFORE, my brother, I implore you by God's mercy to offer your very selves to him, a living sacrifice dedicated and fit for his acceptance, the worship offered by mind and heart. Adapt yourselves no longer to the pattern of this present world, but let your mind be remade and your whole nature thus transformed. Then you will be able to discern the will of God, and to know what is good, acceptable and perfect.

— *Romans 12: 1–2*

SHOW me his friends and I the man shall know;
This wiser turn a larger wisdom lends:
Show me the books he loves and I shall know
The man far better than through mortal friends.

— *Silas Weir Mitchell*

THE HERITAGE BOOK

I HAD a lovely visit today from a young schoolteacher from our local school. She is a primary grade teacher fresh from teacher's training, having graduated last June. Her visit was unexpected but very welcome.

Laurie's class has several children who have behaviour problems and Laurie thinks that she may have an idea to help these children.

"Mrs. McCann, I am asking you and several other grandmothers in the neighbourhood if you could give up one afternoon a week to help me. These children love stories and they need to be cuddled. If you could come and take just one of these children on your knee and read to them I think it will do them the world of good."

I am more than happy to help out as are several friends of mine. Our "job" starts next week. I am looking forward to it with excitement.

WEDNESDAY — SEPTEMBER 27

MY daughter Julia was here for dinner this evening and it was one of the nicest evenings I've had in a very long time. Julia is so busy in her work that we are not able to see her as often as we would like.

She is working with an international corporation and because of this she has travelled extensively. We listened for hours as she told us amusing and interesting stories of her travels.

One of the funniest events occurred in India at a very high-class hotel. As she walked across the opulent marble floor of the lobby a very large rat scurried in front of her. Naturally she was startled into a shriek but when she mentioned it to the desk captain he said "Oh madame, we don't have rodents." And that was the end of that.

THURSDAY — SEPTEMBER 28

ANYONE who has had a bull by the tail knows five or six things more than someone who hasn't.

— *Mark Twain*

THE HERITAGE BOOK

ALTHOUGH I enjoy the advantages of one-stop supermarket shopping there is one thing that I miss very much. It is the smell and the taste of homemade fresh bread. The busy lifestyle of today doesn't allow us the luxury of freshly baked bread every day but there are times when Marg and I miss it enough to spend a day baking.

It's probably just as well for our waistlines that we do this rarely. Bruce, Marg, and I managed to eat one whole loaf at dinner this evening. There really is nothing quite like it!

THE obscure we see eventually — the completely apparent takes a little longer.

— *Edward R. Murrow*

October

I know how to get along with humble means and I know how to live in prosperity in any and every circumstance. I have learned the secret of being filled and going hungry, both of having abundance and suffering need.

I can do all things through Him who strengthens me.

— Philippians 4: 12–13

WE may give without loving, but we cannot love without giving.

THE HERITAGE BOOK

How important it is to try always to be kind. My mother told us this story many times when we were growing up and it never failed to make an impression.

A woman regularly bought her eggs, butter, and milk from a farmer who had an excellent reputation for fine products and prompt delivery.

Then one day when she needed eggs for a special cake the farmer failed to arrive.

On his next delivery day the woman was very harsh in her criticism.

The farmer said quietly "I'm sorry if you were inconvenienced ma'am, but I was attending my father's funeral."

The woman was terribly ashamed and vowed never to be critical until she had heard the other side of any story.

It is certainly a story worth remembering and thinking about.

M ANY people have expressed their opinions about education and I offer you several of these.

Let early education be a sort of amusement; you will then be better able to find out the natural bent.

— *Plato*

If we succeed in giving the love of learning, the learning itself is sure to follow.

— *John Lubbock*

Never discourage anyone who continually makes progress, no matter how slow.

— *Plato*

Don't limit a child to your own learning, for he was born in another time.

— *Rabbinical saying*

When you wish to instruct, be brief; that men's minds take in quickly what you say, learn its lesson, and retain it faithfully. Every word that is unnecessary only pours over the side of a brimming mind.

— *Cicero*

THE HERITAGE BOOK

I spent the afternoon at school today and it was quickly apparent why Laurie had asked for help.

The young lad placed in my care was a real handful. When I told him that we were going out of the room to read a story he announced forcefully, "I hate yucky stories and I don't want to go with you!"

It took several minutes of gentle persuasion before Andrew came with me to the library. Laurie had wisely chosen a very funny book for us to start with. As I began to read Andrew sat on the floor playing with his shoelaces. Shortly, however, he began inching closer and closer until he could see the pictures. It took only a few more minutes before he was perched on my lap and chuckling softly as I read.

By the end of the hour we were getting on quite well. He had difficulty sitting still and he was not inclined to talk much, however I hope that we may change that in the coming weeks.

It does make a person feel good to be needed.

THE HERITAGE BOOK

IF you are wise, you will mingle one thing with the other not hoping without doubt, not doubting without hope.

— *Seneca*

TODAY we went to the country to visit with my grandson Fred and his wife June and their two sons Mickey and Geoffrey.

It was a glorious fall day and we all took a hike back into the woods.

The two boys collected a number of brightly coloured leaves in a bag and when we got back to the house they disappeared for quite some time. When they came down for dinner they presented me with a beautiful leaf collage on black paper.

It was a lovely day with a very tangible object to keep the memory fresh.

LOVE your neighbours as yourself: love cannot wrong a neighbour, therefore the whole law is summed up in love.

— *Romans 13: 10*

THE HERITAGE BOOK

BEGIN; to begin is half the work. Let half still remain; again begin this, and thou wilt have finished.

— Ausonius

O sun and skies and clouds of June,
And flowers of June together,
Ye cannot rival for one hour
October's bright blue weather,

When loud the bumble-bee makes haste,
Belated, thriftless vagrant,
And goldenrod is dying fast,
And lanes with grapes are fragrant;

When comrades seek sweet country haunts,
By twos and twos together,
And count like misers hour by hour,
October's bright blue weather.

O suns and skies and flowers of June
Count all your boasts together,
Love loveth best of all the year
October's bright blue weather.

— Helen Hunt Jackson

THE HERITAGE BOOK

I have always admired people who show courage in the face of adversity. Several years ago a young Canadian lost a leg to cancer. This could easily have made him angry and bitter.

He did become angry, not at his loss, but at the disease that caused it. He decided to start a run across our country in an effort to raise money for cancer research.

In Ontario people came by the thousands to cheer him on as he ran. I will never forget the sight of this one-legged runner as he ran-hopped by me on a warm summer morning in Muskoka.

A year later Terry Fox succumbed to cancer.

"Terry Fox's race is over. In fact he never finished the course; none of us do. What is important is to set goals. What is important is not to quit, not ever. What is important is to run well and honestly, with as much human grace as possible—not forgetting, too, to take joy in the running."

— *The Globe and Mail (July 1, 1981)*

THURSDAY — OCTOBER 12

DEDICATE some of your life to others. Your dedication will not be a sacrifice. It will be an exhilarating experience because it is an intense effort applied to a meaningful end.

— *Dr. Thomas Dooley*

FRIDAY — OCTOBER 13

TODAY we pulled out the dead plants and raked out leaves and debris from the garden.

Many years ago when I complained to my father about all of the work he replied, "Edna, remember that every day's work done in the garden in the fall saves a week's work in the spring." I know that when next April arrives we will be grateful for a clean start.

SATURDAY — OCTOBER 14

SIR Winston Churchill offered this advice on speechmaking to a young Prince of Wales.

"If you have an important point to make, don't try to be subtle or clever. Use a pile driver. Hit the point once. Then come back and hit it again. Then hit it a third time — a tremendous whack."

ALMIGHTY and Gracious Father, we give thanks for the fruits of the earth in their season and for the labour of those who harvest them. Make us, we pray, faithful stewards of your gifts, for the provision of our necessities and the relief of all who are in need, to the glory of your name, through Jesus Christ our Lord who is alive and reigns with you and the Holy Spirit, one God, now and forever. Amen.

WE all have so much for which we are grateful.

The McCanns have always made Thanksgiving a time for family reunion. This year we are expecting about thirty family members and all are bringing their favourite dishes. Marg and Bruce will be cooking a large turkey that was sent to them by a good friend who is a turkey farmer.

This day is a lot of work but I feel that it is worth all of the effort we put into the occasion. Its real value is the renewal of family ties and bonds of love that keep our family close.

TUESDAY — OCTOBER 17

THOU canst begin a new life! See but things afresh as thou used to see them; for in this consists the new life.

— Marcus Aurelius

WEDNESDAY — OCTOBER 18

DEMAND not that events should happen as you wish, but wish them to happen as they do, and you will go on well.

— Epictetus

THURSDAY — OCTOBER 19

SOMEONE once said that October is just the happy side of summer and the pleasant side of winter.

FRIDAY — OCTOBER 20

WE sleep, but the loom of life never stops and the pattern which was weaving when the sun went down is weaving when it comes up tomorrow.

— Henry Ward Beecher

SATURDAY — OCTOBER 21

WORRY is a thin stream of fear trickling through the mind. If encouraged it cuts a channel into which all other thoughts are drained.

— *Arthur Somers Roche*

SUNDAY — OCTOBER 22

THE Lord is near, have no anxiety, but in everything make your request known to God in prayer and petition with thanksgiving. Then the peace of God which is beyond our utmost understanding will keep guard over your hearts and your thoughts, in Christ Jesus.

— *Philippians 4: 6-7*

MONDAY — OCTOBER 23

THE superior man, when resting in safety, does not forget that danger may come. When in a state of security he does not forget the possibility of ruin. When all is orderly, he does not forget that disorder may come. Thus his person is not endangered, and his States and all their clans are preserved.

— *Confucius*

Tuesday — October 24

A retentive memory is a good thing, but the ability to forget is a true sign of greatness.

Wednesday — October 25

England is well known for its rainy weather. My friend Peggy Cay lives in England and she wrote to me of this amusing conversation after a particularly bad spell this past summer.

"Rain, fog, rain, and more fog. When do you people ever have summer?" a visitor to London asked disgustedly. With typical English wit his host replied, "That is quite a difficult question, old boy, but last year I do believe it came on a Wednesday."

Thursday — October 26

October is the month for painted leaves — As fruits and leaves and the day itself acquire a bright tint just before they fall, so the year nears its setting. October is its sunset sky; November the later twilight.

— *Henry David Thoreau*

THE HERITAGE BOOK

MY good friends Will and Muriel stopped by today, eager to tell me the news of their granddaughter Kristen.

Kristen, a ten-year-old, is attending the National Ballet School in Toronto. It has long been regarded as one of the world's leading ballet schools.

The young people here are committed to their art. They need to be. Students work eight to ten hours a day, with three hours of ballet plus the academic subjects required by the Ontario Ministry of Education. Younger students perform in the National Ballet's "The Nutcracker" at Christmas and the entire school has an annual spring concert.

Young Kristen is enjoying every minute at the school. As Veronica Tennant, a prima ballerina and graduate of the school, has said "Your creative talents have been encouraged, and you have received an academic education of the highest calibre. You could not be better prepared for whatever lies ahead."

Autumn's good, a cosy season;
Then there's work for man and woman,
While each day the sunlight dwindles
Speckled fawn through reddening bracken
Scatter from the herd.

Hogs leap up from sandy hollows
Answering the hind's deep bellow,
Acorns dropping in peaceful woodlands,
Corn stands up in golden plenty
Over the brown world.

Even the spiky thorn-bush growing
By the old deserted fortress
Staggers with its weight of berries,
Hazel nuts thud in the forest
From the wearied boughs.
   — *Translated from Irish by Frank O'Connor*

Go before us, O Lord, in all our doings with
thy most gracious favour, and further us
with thy continual help; that in all our works,
begun, continued, and ended in thee, we may
glorify thy holy name, and finally by thy
mercy obtain everlasting life; through Jesus
Christ our Lord.
                    — *Book of Common Prayer*

THE HERITAGE BOOK

AT cool of day, with God I walk
My garden's grateful shade;
I hear His voice among the trees,
And I am not afraid.
   He speaks to me in every wind,
He smiles from every star;
He is not deaf to me, nor blind,
Nor absent, nor afar.
   His hand that shuts the flowers to sleep,
Each in its dewy fold,
Is strong my feeble life to keep,
And competent to hold.
   The powers below and powers above,
Are subject to His care —
I cannot wander from His love
Who loves me everywhere.
   Thus dowered, and guarded thus, with Him
I walked this peaceful shade;
I hear His voice among the trees,
And I am not afraid.

HALLOWE'EN, a special night
To give each one a nasty fright.
The jack-o-lantern's burning well
As tiny witches cast their spell.

November

All Saints Day

Last evening as we said our "Good nights" my son-in-law Bruce said to me, "Edna, tomorrow is All Saints Day. If you would like to go to the celebration of the Eucharist I would like to join you."

Bruce was always very fond of my husband George and since I have made my home with him and Marg, November first has been a time for him and me to go to the Eucharist service at our church.

This morning, in spite of the rainy November-like weather, Bruce and I went to the service to remember a loved one who was truly a "saint" to us.

THE HERITAGE BOOK

As former readers know, November is my least favourite month of the year. I am always looking for ways to make November less dreary and grey. Several of my readers have written to me to offer suggestions and here are some of my favourites.

When you feel blue write a letter to an old friend to tell them of any good news that you may have.

Another reader suggests that you plan to have friends over often for meals in November. She even called a neighbour to come in for breakfast and it lifted her whole day.

"A good fire with a cup of tea" is another of my favourites.

I think the suggestion that I liked the best came from a friend in a nursing home.

"If you feel as grey as the weather why not pay a visit to a local nursing home. The people there would certainly enjoy the company and visiting with some who are less fortunate than you is a sure-fire pick-me-up."

THE HERITAGE BOOK

INGRATITUDE is always a form of weakness. I have never known a man of real ability to be ungrateful.

THERE is a course for families being offered at our library called "Conversation, *not* a lost art." Our librarian remarked that she was surprised by how many signed up for the program. But after thinking about it for some time, I can understand why so many families would need some practice at conversational skills.

We have many conversation substitutes in our homes today: T.V., radio, stereos, and more. Often, as well, both parents are working and times for conversation are few and of short duration.

Nothing is more important than communication, one with another. If this course can provide help with this vital part of our lives it will certainly benefit the participants.

THE HERITAGE BOOK

O most merciful Father, we humbly thank thee for all thy gifts so freely bestowed upon us; for life and health and safety, for power to work and leisure to rest, for all that is beautiful in creation and in the lives of men; but above all we thank thee for our spiritual mercies in Christ Jesus our Lord; who with thee and the Holy Spirit liveth and reigneth, one God, for ever and ever. Amen.

— *Book of Common Prayer*

IT is unfortunate that in the game of life many people are content to be in the bleacher seats.

TUESDAY — NOVEMBER 7

SOMEONE once asked billionaire John Paul Getty to explain his success. Getty summed it up nicely when he said "Some people find oil. Others don't."

WEDNESDAY — NOVEMBER 8

MANY great things are accomplished in the face of adversity. Did you know that Mozart, one of the great musical composers of all time, was unable to afford heat in his room? Some of his most immortal music was written while his hands were wrapped in woolen socks for warmth.

THURSDAY — NOVEMBER 9

THE most powerful weapon on earth is the human soul on fire.

— Ferdinand Foch

THE HERITAGE BOOK

Friday — November 10

DON'T flatter yourself that friendship authorizes you to say disagreeable things to your intimates. The nearer you come into relation with a person, the more necessary do tact and courtesy become. Except in cases of necessity, which are rare, leave your friend to learn unpleasant things from his enemies; they are ready enough to tell them.

— *Oliver Wendell Holmes*

Saturday — November 11

Armistice Day

WHEN we think of Armistice Day these well-known lines of poetry come to mind:

In Flanders fields the poppies blow
Beneath the crosses, row on row.

This immortal poem was written in grief by a young Canadian for a dear friend who had fallen in the battle of Ypres.

SUNDAY — NOVEMBER 12

DEAR Lord, we pray today that our world may live in peace. Where there is a war, let it end; where there is suffering, let there be healing; where there is unhappiness, let there be joy. And this we pray in the name of Jesus Christ, our Lord. Amen.

MONDAY — NOVEMBER 13

MY grandson Marshall is a lawyer and as such has been given endless advice from more experienced colleagues. The advice he enjoyed most was that which he heard given by American Justice Harlan Fiske.

"If you're strong on the facts and weak on the law, discuss the facts. If you're strong on the law and weak on the facts, discuss the law. If you're weak on the law and weak on the facts — bang the table."

TUESDAY — NOVEMBER 14

THE smallest good deed is better than the grandest intention.

THE HERITAGE BOOK

WEDNESDAY — NOVEMBER 15

A kind word is never lost. It keeps going on and on, from one person to another, until at last it comes back to you again.

THURSDAY — NOVEMBER 16

I had a most unusual experience today.

I was going to visit an old friend, Emily, at her apartment in Burlington. I pushed the button in the elevator for the correct floor and the doors slid shut. The car started up but then suddenly it jerked, the lights flickered, stayed on, and upward motion ceased. After I had pushed many buttons with no results a real sense of fear took hold. Then the small phone rang and the friendly voice of the manager assured me that there was a problem but that they were working on it.

For the next two hours I did what I knew would keep my mind occupied and off my incarceration — I tidied my purse.

Eventually, I was released but it was an experience I do not wish to repeat.

FRIDAY — NOVEMBER 17

REFLECT on your present blessings, of which every man has many, not on your past misfortunes, of which all men have some.

— *Charles Dickens*

SATURDAY — NOVEMBER 18

MANY years ago a good friend of ours was beset by financial troubles. As if that weren't enough his wife was in poor health.

George and I were very surprised therefore to see how well he was able to handle this difficult time in his life. His explanation was uplifting.

"Friends," he said, "either all of this will turn out well or God will give me the strength to endure the worst."

SUNDAY — NOVEMBER 19

HOW shall a young man steer an honest course? By holding to thy word. With my whole heart I strive to find thee; let me not stray from thy commandments.

— *Psalm 119: 9–10*

THE HERITAGE BOOK

ONE of the most time-saving devices in the kitchen today is the microwave oven. I assumed that this scientific wonder was a very recent invention, and so was very surprised to learn that it was back in 1945 that scientist Percy L. Spencer first used microwaves to cook.

He happened on the idea by accident. He laid a chocolate bar beside a radium vacuum tube he was testing. Moments later, the candy bar was a melted mess. Next he tested a raw egg and popcorn in front of a small radar horn antenna. The popcorn popped and the egg exploded.

Spencer had discovered to his great surprise that it was possible to cook with microwaves.

The first oven was manufactured in 1947. It sold to hotels and restaurants for about three thousand dollars. In 1967 the first U.S. microwave oven became available for use in homes.

The microwave saves time, energy, and does not heat up the whole kitchen. Bruce gave Marg a microwave oven several years ago and it has been used constantly ever since.

THE HERITAGE BOOK

ONE of my favourite stories of all time is *Anne of Green Gables*, written by Lucy Maud Montgomery.

For eighty-three years now the red-haired, freckle-faced Anne has made her way into the hearts of young girls the world over.

The story was very nearly never published. It had been rejected by five publishers and packed away in a closet in Lucy Maud's small Cavendish home. Then two years later, in 1906, she found the manuscript while rummaging in an old box. As she reread the story she decided to try one more time, and sent the story to L.C. Page and Company of Boston, Massachusetts.

Within six months *Anne of Green Gables* had gone through six editions and readers were begging for more.

Subsequently, Lucy Maud provided *Anne of Avonlea*, *Anne of the Island*, *Anne of Windy Poplars*, *Anne's House of Dreams*, and *Anne of Ingleside*.

The most recent movie version was made for television and starred Megan Follows, a young Canadian actress. She was the perfect Anne and I fell in love again with Anne and Green Gables.

WEDNESDAY — NOVEMBER 22

WHEN you encounter difficulties and con-
tradictions, do not try to break them, but
bend them with gentleness and time.

— Saint Francis de Sales

THURSDAY — NOVEMBER 23

TODAY is the Thanksgiving holiday for our
neighbours to the south.

Of the 102 pilgrims who set forth on the
Mayflower, only 51 sat down to the first
Thanksgiving dinner in 1621. The other half of
the group lay buried on a nearby hill, victims
of disease and privation.

In spite of this the pilgrims had cause to be
thankful — for an abundant harvest, new
homes, and friendly Indians.

It is a good thing to give thanks unto the
Lord.

— Psalm 92: 1

FRIDAY — NOVEMBER 24

TODAY is the tomorrow you worried about
yesterday.

Saturday — November 25

During World War II there was a special prayer that was said in the air raid shelters of England.

"Increase of God, the spirit of neighbourliness among us, that in peril we may uphold one another, in calamity serve one another, in suffering tend one another and in homelessness and loneliness in exile befriend one another. Grant us brave and enduring hearts that we may strengthen one another, till the disciplines and testing of these days be ended, and thou dost give again peace in our time through Jesus Christ, our Lord. Amen."

Sunday — November 26

We know that all things work together for good to them that love God, to them who are called according to his purpose.

— *Romans 8: 28*

THE HERITAGE BOOK

As the weather turns colder ice will begin to form on the Rideau Canal. The canal will become the longest skating rink in the world, with close to nine kilometres of well-kept ice.

The canal was built between 1826 and 1832. Its original intent was to provide a safe inland passage from Montreal to Lake Ontario and Kingston.

In order to climb the 84 metres to overcome a massive hump of Precambrian Shield and then drop 49 metres to Lake Ontario, it was necessary to construct 47 locks and 30 control dams in what has been called one of the greatest engineering works of the last century.

Today thousands of skaters use the canal as a route from home to the office. In the spring and summer the skaters become boaters, with some 5000 boaters yearly on the 200-kilometre route between Ottawa and Kingston.

Winter or summer it is a great source of pleasure in Ottawa.

THE HERITAGE BOOK

STRANGE that I did not know him then,
That friend of mine!
I did not even show him then
One friendly sign;

But cursed him for the ways he had
To make me see
My envy of the praise he had
For praising me.

I would have rid the earth of him
Once in my pride —
I never knew the worth of him
Until he died.

IF this invisible germ of life in the grain of
wheat can thus pass unimpaired through
three thousand resurrections, I shall not doubt
that my soul has power to clothe itself with a
new body, suited to a new existence, when this
early frame has crumbled into dust.

— William Jennings Bryan

Thursday — November 30

L ORD Baden Powell, as you probably know, was the founder of the Boy Scouts.

It is not a well-known story but when Baden Powell died in Kenya in 1941, the Dean of Westminster wrote to Lady Baden Powell offering her a place of honour in Westminster Abbey for her husband.

Although the family was deeply moved by the offer they knew that Baden Powell, a modest man, would want a simpler end. And so it was that he was borne to his final resting place, by soldiers and scouts, in a small Kenyan cemetery.

On the stone bearing his name, under the dates of birth and death, is carved a circle with a dot in the centre.

Every scout in the world would recognize immediately the sign, for to a scout it means simply, "I have gone home."

December

IT'S the little things in life that count,
The things of every day;
Just the simple things that we can do,
The kind words we can say.
The little things like a friendly smile
For those who may be sad,
The clasp of a hand or kindly deed
To help make someone glad.
A knock on the door of lonely homes,
Or flowers bright and gay,
For someone to whom you might bring cheer
With just a small bouquet.
Just the little greetings here and there
On which so much depends,
The little pleasures that all can share,
The joy of making friends.

THE HERITAGE BOOK

SATURDAY — DECEMBER 2

As a young child I loved to read. I was greatly encouraged in this endeavour by my parents. Both my mother and my father were very well read and we had a vast collection of books that were available to us whenever we chose to read them. Many of our friends' parents were very critical of the fact that our reading was never censored. They felt that we were often reading works that should have been forbidden to us.

My parents were adamant however and we were allowed to read whatever we chose. I think their decision was sound. Many of the books that were forbidden to our friends were the ones that we decided, on our own, that we didn't want to read.

Reading has been a great joy in my life and I thank my parents for this.

SUNDAY — DECEMBER 3

Come thou long expected Jesus
Born to set thy people free:
From our fears and sin release us,
Let us find our rest in thee.

— Charles Wesley

MONDAY — DECEMBER 4

As to your method of work — take no thought for the morrow. Live neither in the past nor in the future, but let each day's work absorb your entire energies, and satisfy your widest ambition.

— Cromwell

TUESDAY — DECEMBER 5

You gain strength, courage and confidence by every experience in which you really stop to look fear in the face. You are able to say to yourself, "I lived through this horror. I can take the next thing that comes along." . . . You must do the thing you think you cannot do.

— Eleanor Roosevelt

WEDNESDAY — DECEMBER 6

Speak clearly, if you speak at all;
Carve every word before you let it fall.

— Oliver Wendell Holmes Jr.

THE HERITAGE BOOK

TODAY Margaret and I enjoyed the day in a charming small town near Paris, Ontario.

St. George is a picturesque spot right on Highway 5 about an hour's drive from our home. Most of the stores on the town's main street are small antique shops filled with beautiful pieces of early Canadiana. The town hall and municipal offices are located in an old Victorian house, also on Main Street. This building has been kept in magnificent condition. We enjoyed seeing how well this town has kept its turn of the century charm.

At noon we ate in a small restaurant in the centre of town. "Twinklebones" is a charming little place. All the food on their menu is home cooked in the back of the restaurant. It was a delicious break in our day.

For any of you that enjoy a change of pace the town of St. George would be a delightful outing.

THE HERITAGE BOOK

CHRISTIE, a friend of my granddaughter Phyllis, is a teacher in a primary class. She had this amusing story for us today.

Young Jimmy was having a very difficult time getting ready to go home. His snowpants were on backwards and his boots were still sitting on the floor. Christie took pity on this tired youngster and sat him on a chair to help him get his boots on. Christie pushed, tugged, and yanked to get the boots on over Jimmy's shoes.

At last the boots were on. "Now Jimmy, where are your mitts?" asked Christie tiredly.

With a resigned little sigh Jimmy replied, "They're in my boots, teacher."

MY great-grandson Mickey has made me a beautiful wooden feeder for the winter birds. This morning I filled the feeder with wild bird seed and small suet balls.

I shall rest easier tonight knowing that at least some of my feathered friends have eaten well.

Sunday — December 10

About this time John the Baptist appeared as a preacher in the Judean wilderness; his theme was Repent, for the Kingdom of heaven is upon you! It is of him that the prophet Isaiah spoke when he said "A voice crying aloud in the wilderness, 'Prepare a way for the Lord, clear a straight path for him.'"

— Matthew 3: 1–3

Monday — December 11

With the holiday season approaching it is a time to think of those less fortunate than we. This can be a very depressing time of year for those who are shut in.

My daughter Mary and her husband John spend many hours visiting the nursing home in their parish and the elderly residents are overjoyed to have their company.

This year the young people of their congregation have organized a special outing to a nearby mall. Special vans to accommodate wheelchairs will take all those residents who are able to see the lights and to Christmas shop.

It takes so little but it means so much.

THE HERITAGE BOOK

THE lives of all of us have been made rich by the many people whom we have known and loved. At this season a card or a note renews that friendship and buoys our spirits with love.

THIS morning a floral delivery van arrived at our house and began unloading poinsettia plants for Margaret and me. First there was a magnificent poinsettia tree, at least three feet tall and nearly as large in diameter. Next came several large red plants and then several more white ones.

Marg and I asked the delivery man if he were not making an error but he said that they were indeed for us.

The card read simply, "With much love from a friend."

I don't know who our "friend" is but our home is resplendent in magnificent red and white poinsettias and I offer my thanks.

THE HERITAGE BOOK

<u>THURSDAY — DECEMBER 14</u>

THERE are no times like the old times —
They shall never be forgot;
There is no place like the old place —
Keep green the dear old spot!
There are no friends like the old friends—
May heaven prolong their lives!
There are no loves like the old loves, —
God bless our loving wives!
— *Oliver Wendell Holmes*

<u>FRIDAY — DECEMBER 15</u>

TODAY was our annual church Christmas bazaar. Marg, Bruce, and I went over early to help decorate and set up the displays.

There were handicrafts of all types, from pine cone wreaths to hand-knit baby sweaters. There were home-made jams, jellies, and relishes as well as home-baked Christmas cookies and plum puddings.

There was a draw for a large gingerbread house, beautifully decorated in icing and gumdrops. Our minister drew the winning ticket and imagine our surprise when my great-grandson Geoffrey was the winner. It was a truly wonderful day.

THE HERITAGE BOOK

I accept this award with an abiding faith in America and an audacious faith in the future of mankind. I refuse to accept the idea that the "isness" of man's present nature makes him morally incapable of reaching up for the "oughtness" that forever confronts him.

— *Martin Luther King, Jr. (accepting the Nobel Peace Prize, 1964)*

THE advent of our God
    With eager prayers we greet,
And singing haste upon his road
His coming reign to meet.

The everlasting Son
Came down to make us free
And He a servant's form put on
To gain our liberty.

— *Charles Coffin*

WHEN a young child was asked to comment on her parents' rather noisy party the youngster remarked "Gee, it's almost like being on our school bus."

THE HERITAGE BOOK

MARSHALL and Jamie Ann stopped by to-night with something very special.

Jamie's parents are now living in Europe and are unable to be here for Christmas. They have sent a video cassette of the family for us to see.

It was wonderfully done! At first Jamie's father strode up the walkway to their home, pointing out the garden and the neighbours' houses. All the while he was chatting just as naturally as if we had been walking up the pathway with him.

As the front door opened Jamie's mother and her two sisters were there bidding us welcome. We were given a quick tour of their home and then the family sat down in the living room and began to relate stories of events as they had happened during the past six months.

Several times Jamie had to wipe the tears away. It was as if we had been sitting with them in their home.

The wonders of technology have made one young lady's Christmas a very happy one.

THE HERITAGE BOOK

THIS evening we attended the nearby school's Christmas concert. I was invited to attend by the children with whom I worked this fall.

It was a wonderful evening. All of the primary classes performed and I know how much work went into the production.

As is usual when young children perform there were a number of small and amusing errors. A snowman's felt carrot nose refused to stay attached to the wearer's own tiny nose and an angel lost her halo three times. The third time, as she bent to retrieve it, several other angels fell over her and caused quite a pile-up. These things of course only added to the audience's enjoyment.

Later, Andrew, the young lad with whom I spent a great deal of time, presented me with a gift that he had made himself—a handpainted bookmark.

WINTER has come and the trees are now bare,
You feel all her wrath on the cold frosty air.

THE HERITAGE BOOK

A wise old gentleman in his eighties gives this advice to friends as they reach sixty.

"You have spent sixty years in preparation for life; you will now begin to live. At sixty you have learned what is worthwhile. You have conquered the worst forms of foolishness. You have reached a "balance" period of life, knowing good from evil, what is precious, what is worthless. Danger is past, the mind is peaceful, evil is forgiven, the affections are strong, envy is weak. It is the happy age."

THE HERITAGE BOOK

FOR many people, today is a time for last-minute shopping. Since I had finished all my shopping and wrapping I decided to take out some old photograph albums of past happy Christmas times.

I could not have had a better day. Christmas was always a wonderfully happy time of family gathering and each and every picture evoked wonderful memories of the loved ones in my life.

SUNDAY — DECEMBER 24

THE virgin will conceive and bear a son, and he shall be called Emmanuel — God is with us.

— Matthew 1:23

MONDAY — DECEMBER 25

FOR unto us a child is born, unto us a son is given: and the government shall be upon his shoulders, and his name shall be called Wonderful Counsellor, Mighty God, Everlasting Father, The Prince of Peace.

— Isaiah 9: 6

TUESDAY — DECEMBER 26

H ARK the herald angels sing,
"Glory to the new-born king."
Peace on earth and mercy mild,
God and sinners reconciled.

— Charles Wesley

WEDNESDAY — DECEMBER 27

A MONG the most popular Christmas decora-
tions are pine cones used in their natural
state or sprayed with Christmas colours of
green and red or silver and gold.

The use of the pine cone is explained in an
old German legend.

A poor woman climbed a mountain to pick
pine cones for fuel. Under the tree was a small
elf who told her to take only the pine cones
from under that one tree.

The woman picked only those cones and
when she arrived home she found that they
had all turned to pure silver. That is why we
use silver cones today.

THURSDAY — DECEMBER 28

T ACT is the ability to close your mouth before someone else wants to.

L IFE, believe, is not a dream
So dark as sages say;
Oft a little morning rain
Foretells a pleasant day.

— Charlotte Brontë

A s yet another year passes it seems like a good time to sit back and reflect on all that we have to be grateful for.

Health, the love of friends and family, and happiness in the small joys of everyday living are but a few of the things that make our lives complete.

M AY I wish for all of you a very happy New Year!